Excel Macros

VBA Programming for Beginners Part 1

By Vijay Kumar

Copyright © 2018 Vijay Kumar

Table of Contents

Introduction

What is an Excel Macro and why you should master it?

Macro is a set of instructions written in VBA (Visual Basic for Applications language). These instructions execute when you run the Macro. For example, using VBA you can make sales report to the Manager in the format he wants in seconds. All the formatting can be done with the help of macro within seconds. Also using VBA, you can make your own keyboard shortcut or Function which is not in the Excel functions list.

Knowing VBA will give wings to you that you have never dreamed of.

If you don't know Excel VBA, you are using Excel like a Car, but Excel is a space shuttle which you are not aware of. So let us learn how to use Excel like a Space shuttle.

How to use this book

I have uploaded all the example files on my site ExceltoVba.com. You can download it from My Ebooks link. It is in a zip format and for unzipping you can use any free unzipping file utility like 7 zip or the proprietary one.

Examples folders have all the files for you to do the exercise specified in the book.

My Assumptions about you.

I assume that you are using Excel for some time and know how to use a filter, to create a chart or pivot table or to write a formula. If you are an absolute beginner in Excel, then you should acquire basic knowledge in Excel before reading this book.

Knowing VBA will be the biggest asset if you are daily interacting with Excel. All the repetitive jobs as well the data manipulation can be done in seconds.

Suggestions for this book

I have taken great care in writing this book to eliminate all the errors in the working examples and the theory part. Still, if you find any error or if you have any suggestions for this book, please send a mail to **vijay@exceltovba.com** with the subject line Errors and Suggestions.

Please write to me for more examples or if you want to cover some more topics I have left out. I will include those topics in the next revision of this book. My ultimate goal is the person who buys this book should get his value for money.

What I want from you.

I want these promises from you before reading the book.

1. You should go through all the example files in this book to understand how VBA is working. I want you to type all the codes instead of copying from the example files provided. If you type, you will understand more about the concepts used in the Programming language and will learn faster. The difference between a novice and expert programmer is the experience he gained from writing programs and learning new concepts. And I want you to have that experience in the shortest time possible.

2. Don't try to learn VBA in one night or you will burn out and throw away this book. My recommendation is to learn at least one or two hour maximum per day continuously till you finish this book. In this way, you will learn much faster. If you have any previous experience in programming, then you can learn quickly.

3. This book should be read from the first chapter to last.

4. Also please give a positive review on Amazon about this book with a five-star rating if possible.

Chapter 1

What is VBA?

Visual Basic for Applications (VBA) is the programming language from Microsoft used for creating Macros and Excel applications. So when you hear VBA or Macro, it refers to the same thing. A macro is an action or a set of actions that you can use to automate tasks. You can always run a macro by clicking the Macros command on the ribbon. VBA is integrated to Excel as well as other Office products so that you can make your programs.

In VBA you don't have to install any additional software as you can write the programs right away in Excel. You only need to install Excel on your computer.

Compared to other programming languages like Java, VBA is easy to learn (but will take some time to master it). Believe me; everyone can make one or two macros on your own without having any programming knowledge. Small repetitive tasks can be recorded using the macro recorder in the Excel without even writing or understanding a single line of code. And the beauty is you can also assign a shortcut of your choice and use it.

VBA Programming

From here on what I am going to say is the primary things required for VBA programming. So please don't stop reading when you feel that you didn't get the concepts correctly. Whatever ideas you didn't grasp today you will understand later in the chapters. If you reread the same chapter two or three times, you will understand more with each reading. Till chapter 4 it is mostly theory and you may feel bored, but don't stop reading. From Chapter 5 fun begins. My personal opinion is after finishing this book, again reread the chapters from first to last and you will understand the chapters better.

Excel Objects

Excel has so many built-in objects. They can receive instructions to do what they are built for by making use of their methods and properties. In Excel, the first object is the application Excel itself (and in Word, it will be Word) followed by other objects in a hierarchical order. Every object may have methods and properties which you can make use of to write programs.

You may be surprised to know, whatever you were using in Excel be it a Pivot table or Chart is an Object. Just imagine if Pivot or Chart is an object then you can instruct Excel to create a Chart or Pivot table for you instead of you creating it manually. For Example, if you want to delete a range of cells from A1:A10, you can write **Range("A1:A10").Delete**. Delete is a method of range object which you can use for deleting. Like that, so many methods and properties are there for each object and you should understand a little bit of each major objects. The rest you can find out quickly from the Excel help menu.

If you don't understand what I have just said, don't worry you will know once you go through next chapters.

Developer Tab

To write macros, you have to enable the Developer Tab in Excel. By default, Developer Tab will not be visible in Excel. You have to enable it. Select Customize Ribbon from Excel Options and put a tick beside the Developer tab to view the Developer Tab in Excel for Excel 2010, 2013 and 2016. Or else, you can right-click on the ribbon and select Customize the ribbon. See the image below.

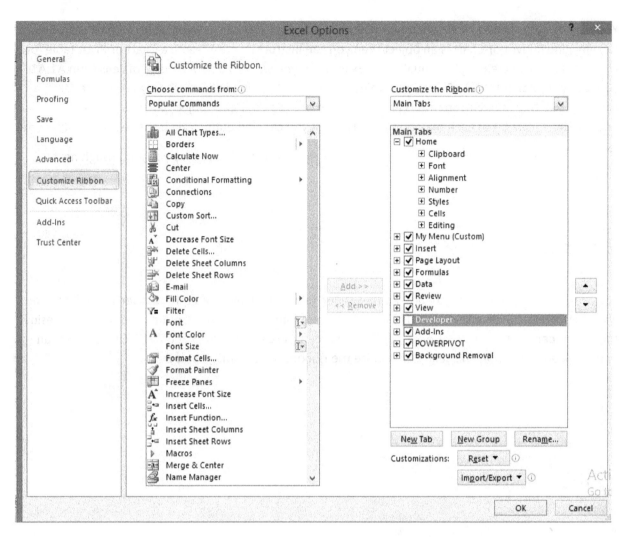

Once enabled you can see the Developer Tab along with other Tabs in Excel. See the image below after it is enabled.

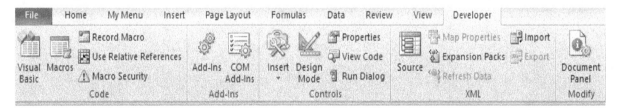

For Excel 2007 you have to click Excel Options under Office button left top , select popular and put a tick mark against **Show Developer Tab in the Ribbon.**

Security Settings for Macros

If you have written a Macro and shared it with your colleague, it may not work on his or her computer due to security reasons. Microsoft has introduced macro security in Excel 2007 to prevent the misuse of the VBA code. Macros can do considerable damage to the computer by deleting specific files or folders or sending unauthorized information through the mail. In other words, it can be used as a virus.

Because of this Security concern Microsoft has given four options to choose the Security you want. You can check the same under File > Option > Trust Center > Trust Center Settings > Macro Settings (in Excel 2010, 2013 and 2016) and it is under Excel Options under Office button (left top

 in Excel 2007.

Four options are given below.

1. **Disable all macros without notification:** If this radio button is selected Macros will not work at all irrespective of what you do, it is permanently disabled.

2. **Disable all macros with notification:** If this radio button is selected, when you open an Excel sheet you will get a Message bar with an option to click and enable the Macros. Or if the Visual Basic Editor window is open, you'll get a message asking if you want to enable Macros.

3. **Disable all macros except digitally signed macros:** If this radio button is selected macros with a digital signature are allowed to run without any problem. But if you have not marked those digital signatures as trusted, then you will get the security warning.

4. **Enable all macros:** If this radio button is selected all the Macros will get executed, in other words, there will not be any security warnings.

By default, Excel uses the Disable All Macros with Notification option.

If you do receive any file containing Macros from outside your organization or from an unknown person by mail, don't open it immediately. Verify the source and then open it, it may have malicious code.

Creating Trusted Folder for the Macros

You can create a trusted folder to store the Excel files containing macros if you are sure they are safe. Also, you can save the one you receive from a trustworthy source in this trusted folder. In this way, you don't have to switch to less secure macro settings. Excel will not give the security warning for the files opened from the trusted folder and macro is enabled on opening.

You should create this folder on your local drive instead of a network drive for safety reasons. If it is in a network computer, somebody can tamper with the files and or add new files without your knowledge.

In Excel go to Excel options and click Trust Center, click Trust Center Settings, and then click Trusted Locations. Here you can see all the default locations and also if you want you can add your locations.

Chapter 2

Your first Macro

Recording your own macro

Excel has a built-in macro recorder to record the actions you are doing in Excel. Then those actions are converted to VBA codes. So without understanding the code, you can make small macros.

For that, first, we will record a small Macro to give all borders to cell A1. Please follow the steps given below.

Step 1: Select Developer Tab > Macros and click on Record Macro. You will get a popup like this.

First one is the Macro name Macro1. You can give any meaningful name but for the time being, don't change it. Shortcut key is the keyboard shortcut which you can assign. Click on the check box after Ctrl+ and press Shift key and R, you will get the shortcut Ctrl + Shift + R. Third one is where to Store macro in, let it be This Workbook.

If you want to describe what your Macro is capable of, you can give a small description in the description box.

Click ok, and the Record Macro Popup will disappear and now whatever you are doing in the Excel sheet will get recorded. You can see a square Stop Recording button on your status bar showing the recording is on.

Step 2: Select cell A1 and select All Borders under Home Tab.

Step 3: Now stop the recording by clicking Stop Recording under Macros in Developer Tab. Or click stop button (square one) in the status bar to stop recording the macro.

Congratulations you have just recorded your first Macro.

Inspecting the macro recorded

Now click on view macros under Macros. You can see the name Macro1 you have just recorded (if someone has recorded a macro before, then you may see the file name as Macro2 or Macro3. Click Macro1 and click the edit button. Another Window will open where you can see the code you have recorded. This new window is Visual Basic Editor (henceforth we will refer to as VBE) where you can see the code you have recorded. Will be going through VBE in detail in the following chapters.

The code you have just recorded will be something like the one given below.

Sub Macro1()

```
' Macro1 Macro
  Range("A1").Select
  Selection.Borders(xlDiagonalDown).LineStyle = xlNone
  Selection.Borders(xlDiagonalUp).LineStyle = xlNone
  With Selection.Borders(xlEdgeLeft)
    .LineStyle = xlContinuous
    .ColorIndex = 0
    .TintAndShade = 0
    .Weight = xlThin
  End With
  With Selection.Borders(xlEdgeTop)
    .LineStyle = xlContinuous
    .ColorIndex = 0
    .TintAndShade = 0
    .Weight = xlThin
  End With
  With Selection.Borders(xlEdgeBottom)
    .LineStyle = xlContinuous
    .ColorIndex = 0
    .TintAndShade = 0
    .Weight = xlThin
```

```
    End With
    With Selection.Borders(xlEdgeRight)
      .LineStyle = xlContinuous
      .ColorIndex = 0
      .TintAndShade = 0
      .Weight = xlThin
    End With
    With Selection.Borders(xlInsideVertical)
      .LineStyle = xlContinuous
      .ColorIndex = 0
      .TintAndShade = 0
      .Weight = xlThin
    End With
    With Selection.Borders(xlInsideHorizontal)
      .LineStyle = xlContinuous
      .ColorIndex = 0
      .TintAndShade = 0
      .Weight = xlThin
    End With

End Sub
```

Yes I know what you are thinking, you have just put a border around a cell and the Macro recorder has thrown up with thirty or forty lines of code. All these codes are not required for putting a border. But Macro recorder has considered other properties also while recording. In your Excel you may not see the exact code as given here, your code may differ according to the version of Excel and is completely ok. Now we can edit the above code and change the same to a single line of code like this.

```
Sub Macro1()
Range("A1").Borders.LineStyle = True
End Sub
```

As you can see that forty lines of codes are not required for putting a border. That is why it is very very important to understand the VBA language to write efficient and readable codes which you can reuse in various projects.

But don't underestimate the power of macro recorder either. You will get a ton of information from the macro recorder. You will learn about new Objects, their methods and properties from macro recorder which you are not aware of by recording. If you don't know how to program for a particular task, record a macro of what you want to do. Then inspect the code to get an idea about the methods and properties used by the recorder. And then you can tweak it according to your need.

To run a Macro recorded

If you want to test run this macro, first remove the borders you have put around A1 cell. Then go back to the VBE and click anywhere inside the code of the macro you have recorded now and press F5 to run this Macro.

Or else you can use these methods to run the Macro.

1. Select Macros > View Macro from View Tab and then select the Macro name you have recorded and click run.

2. Use the shortcut key Alt + F11 or click Visual Basic under Developer Tab to open the VBE editor. Press F5 or click Play button icon in the Standard Toolbar while the cursor is inside the Macro you want to run. If your cursor is not inside any Code, it will give a pop up with all the macro names and you can select the Macro you want to Run.

3. You can use the shortcut you have assigned to all the Macro.

4. Or use the Run menu and click run

Important note: At this stage, if you run this macro it will get executed in the active sheet. Means if you have opened two or three Excel files the macro will execute in the last opened Excel book. Also, keep in mind the macro once executed cannot be undone. In other words, there is no undo key.

Absolute and Relative mode of recording

There are two modes of recording, one is Absolute and the other one is Relative, default one is Absolute. What we have just recorded is in Absolute reference. If you run this macro once again irrespective of the cell you are, it will always put the border to A1 cell. Recording in Absolute mode is not at all useful in most of the cases as it will always refer to the same cell.

Select Sheet2 and run the macro by clicking the shortcut assigned earlier Ctrl + Shift + R or use any of the other methods given in the previous section.

Now we will again record the same in Relative mode. Please follow these steps.

Step 1. First select View > Macro > and Select Relative reference.

Step 2. Now click the record macro button and give the macro name as Relative.

Step 3. Now put the border around A1 and stop the recording.

Step 4. Now select any other cell and run the Relative macro you have just recorded, the cell you have selected will get the Border around it. This macro is handy, try selecting another cell or group of cells and run the macro to get a border around the cell or cells you have chosen.

Editing the Macro

For Editing the Macro, you can select the Macros from View Tab and select the Macro name you have created and then click edit. You will be taken directly to the code window of the Macro you have chosen.

Procedures declared as private will not be visible in the Macros window (more about that in the coming chapters). Or else you can go directly to the code window by selecting Visual basic from the Developer tab and click the Module1 in the Project Window to see the code (If Project window is not visible select view > Project Explorer from VBE).

Record small repetitive tasks.

Now try recording these macros to get the hang of how you can record simple macros and give a Keyboard shortcut for the same. For recording these simple macros, you don't want to learn VBA as Macro recorder will automatically generate the code for you. After recording these macros go through the codes you have recorded.

1. We want to make the First row bold and font to Red. First, start recording the macro by giving a shortcut and then select the first row and make it bold and font to Red and stop the macro. Now go to sheet two and enter some data in the first row and click the shortcut assigned or directly execute from VBE by selecting the macro recorded.

2. Make the background color of a cell to Green.

3. If you have a file having ten columns delete the first five columns and view the code recorded.

Macro Recorder Advantage and Limitations

Macro recorder is useful for generating straight and simple repetitive tasks. But macro recorder cannot be used for complex programming like loops, pop up messages or calculating values according to your inputs. For that, you have to write procedures and I will help you understand and write this kind of codes.

As I said before Macro Recorder is very useful in another way. When you are writing codes with unknown objects, you can find out the methods or properties by recording and inspecting the code after that. It will provide new methods and properties of the objects which you are not familiar with. I used to do this all the time and almost all the programmers use this trick.

If you are not sure how to start programming for a particular task, the best way is to record a macro and find out what codes you are getting. You will find some ideas for sure. Then you can edit the code generated to your need and once satisfied with the code behavior you can use it in your main procedure.

Saving the file with Macros

Excel will not allow saving the macros directly in the Excel files saving with .xls or .xlsx extension due to security reasons from Excel 2007. You have to use the macro-enabled workbooks file extension xlsm. Another option is, you can create a Personal Macro Workbook so that every time you open an Excel file, this will also open with all the macros you have saved.

For that when you record a Macro, you can select store macro in as Personal Macro Workbook and click OK. Once the macro is recorded, it is saved in the Personal Macro Workbook. By default, the Personal macro file is not there in Excel. It is created the first time when you opt to save the same in the Personal workbook. So next time when you open an Excel file Personal workbook will also open. You can store all the small useful macros in the Personal workbook.

For creating a Personal Macro Workbook follow these steps.

1. Select Macros – Record Macro.

2. Give a macro name Personal and select store macro in as Personal Macro Workbook and click OK.

3. Again select Macros and click stop recording.

4. Now in the View tab click unhide to unhide the Personal.xlsb file.

5. Now got to Macros and click view macros. Select Personal and click edit to see the macro you have created; it begins with **Sub Personal** and ends with **End Sub.**

6. Delete **Personal** (whole content) and copy these two macros Sub Border(), Sub Width_Coloumn_correction()given below and paste it in the place of **Personal** and click save and close the Visual Editor (should copy from Sub to End sub individually)

This one will create a border around the cell or cells you have selected when you press the keys Ctrl+Shift+B

Sub Border()

' Keyboard Shortcut: Ctrl+Shift+B

Selection.Borders.LineStyle = True

End Sub

This one will automatically adjust the width of the column according to the length of the text in the column.

Sub Width_Coloumn_correction()

' Keyboard Shortcut: Ctrl+Shift+W

Cells.EntireColumn.AutoFit

Range("A1").Select

End Sub

7. After that select Macros – View Macros and select Border macro. Then click options and use Shift + B to assign the shortcut Ctrl+Shift+B. Like that assign the shortcut Ctrl+Shift+W to Width_Column_Correction macro.

8. Again hide the Personal.xlsb file from View tab and save the Excel file and exit.

Next time when you open any Excel file, these shortcuts will be there for you to use. Try out these shortcuts.

Instead of hiding and unhiding the personal workbook you can go directly to the Visual Basic editor. Then click Visual Basic from Developer tab and select the personal workbook. You will see a file named Personal.XLSB which is the personal workbook you have just created.

Chapter 3

Visual Basic Editor (VBE)

Visual Basic Editor or VBE is a separate application which resides in Excel where you write and edit all your Macros. You cannot open VBE separately; it can be opened only when an Excel file is open. If you want to open VBE, you can use the shortcut Alt+F11 while in Excel or you can click open the Visual Basic from the Developer Tab. Now open the VBE, you will get a screen like this as seen in the image given below. What each subsection is used is explained in the coming section.

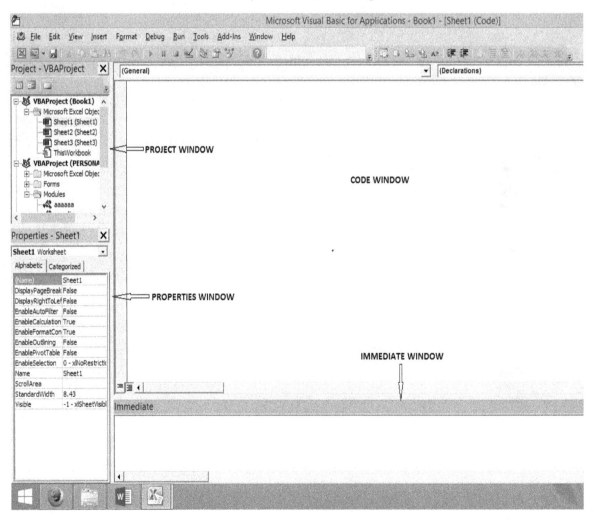

Project Explorer

The Project Explorer lists any open workbooks and add-ins that are loaded. If the Project Explorer is not visible select view menu and select Project Explorer. If you click the + icon next to the VBA Project, you will see a folder called Microsoft Excel objects. This node expands to show an item for each sheet in the workbook (each sheet is considered an object), and another object called ThisWorkbook (which represents the Workbook object). Code specific to the sheet is stored in the sheet modules and the Workbook events are placed in the ThisWorkbook module.

If the project has any VBA modules, the project listing also shows a Modules node. There can also be folders for forms and class modules. Each folder includes one or more individual components.

To insert a new module, right-click the project, and then choose the type of module you want. These are the available modules.

Forms - You can make your own forms in Excel to get information from the user. You can make a form to collect the employee information like first name, second name, DOB, etc.

Modules - Standard modules are where you store almost all the codes. When you record a macro, the codes will be placed inside these modules. Each module can hold up to 64000 characters. So basically you can have as many modules and procedures as you wish.

Class modules - Class modules are used to create your own objects.

Right-clicking a component and selecting View Code or double-clicking the components brings up any code in the Programming window. The exception is userforms, where double-clicking displays the userform in Design view.

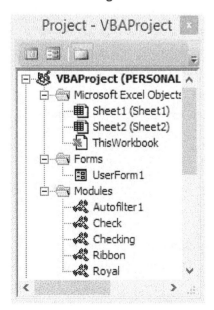

Here on the image, you can see Sheet1 and Sheet2. Those are the Sheet1 and Sheet2 objects. If you double click those two the corresponding code window will open and you can write code related to those objects. Keep in mind the codes written in the sheet1 will work only for sheet1. If you want the codes to work on all sheets, then you should write the codes in modules.

Also, you can see a Folder named Forms and a user form called UserForm1. This is actually a user form created and if you double click, you will get the user form window in design mode.

Under that, you can see the Modules Folder and the different modules I have created. By default, the module names will be like Module1, Module2 and so on, here I have renamed it. You should rename them from the Properties window to quickly identify the Projects and for better maintainability. Usually, I put the codes in different modules according to usage or department wise or project wise.

Code Window

Code window is where you will write all the codes. Each worksheet will have its own code window. So if you click the sheet1 in Project Explorer, the code window pertains to sheet1 will open, likewise for sheet2 and sheet3. And each module will have its own code window.

You can get the Code window by using the shortcut F7 or select Code from the view menu from VBE. You will get the Code window corresponding to the object you have selected.

If already the code window is opened then you have to click the object directly to get the code window of that object.

Properties Window

Properties window holds the properties of the Object. If you select sheet1 object in the Project Window, it will show sheet1 properties and for sheet2 it will show the sheet2 properties. If user form is there, it will show the user form properties. If the properties window is not visible, you can select the properties window from view menu or else you can use the shortcut F4. As discussed earlier you can rename the module from the Properties window.

Immediate Window

You can get the immediate window by pressing CTRL + G or select Immediate Window from the view menu. Immediate window will execute the VBA statements you enter in that window. We will discuss more about immediate window in the later chapters and its uses.

Customizing VBE Editor

You will be working in VBE editor for most of the time and if you want to make some customization, you can select options from the tools menu. You can see a dialog box with four tabs: Editor, Editor Format, General, and Docking. We will explore some of the options found on each tab.

The Editors Tab

Given below is the image when Editors Tab is selected.

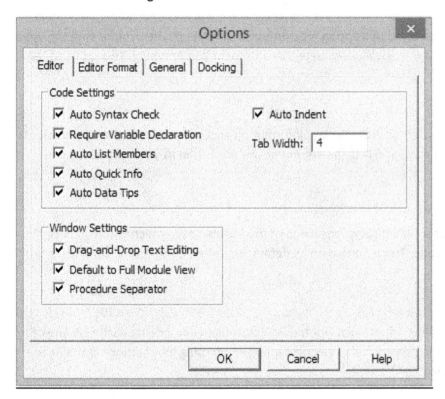

Auto Syntax Check: This option will check for any syntax error and pops up a dialogue box while entering the VBA code. The dialogue will tell you roughly what the problem is. If you don't select this options syntax errors will be highlighted in a different color other than the code.

For beginners, you can keep this on to get details about the errors. All experienced programmers will turn this off as it will pop up error messages now and then and will slow you down. I can identify the errors quickly without this option most of the time.

Require Variable Declaration: If this option is selected, VBE inserts the statement **Option Explicit** at the beginning of each new VBA module you insert. Changing this setting affects only new modules, not existing modules. If this statement appears in your module, you must explicitly define each variable you use using a Dim statement.

This option should always be selected to force you to declare the variable. It is crucial for debugging as well as to have tight control of the program you write. Also if you explicitly declare the variable, it will not behave in any other way. If the variable is not declared, by default, it is a variant, which can store any data type and it will change the data type by the data you assign to the variable. It will slow down the program. If the variable is declared VBE knows the data type and assigns that much memory and program will run fast.

Auto List Members: If you have selected this option, VBE provides some help when you're entering your VBA code. It displays a list that would logically complete the statement you're typing. This is one of the best features in VBE.

Auto Quick Info: If this option is selected, VBE displays information about functions and their arguments as you type. This is similar to the way Excel lists the arguments for a function as you start typing a new formula.

Auto Data Tips: If this option is set, VBE displays the value of the variable over which your cursor is placed when you're debugging code. This is turned on by default and often quite useful. Don't ever turn this option off.

Auto Indent: The Auto Indent setting determines whether VBE automatically indents each new line of code the same as the previous line. Most Excel developers are keen on using indentations in their code, so this option is typically kept on.

Drag-and-Drop Text Editing: This option when selected lets you copy and move text by dragging and dropping with your mouse.

Default to Full Module View: If this is selected, procedures in the Code window appear as a single scrollable list. If this option is turned off, you can see only one procedure at a time.

Procedure Separator: When this option is selected, separator bars appear at the end of each procedure in a Code window. Separator bars provide a nice visual line between procedures, making it easy to see where one piece of code ends and where another starts.

Editor Format tab

The figure below shows the Editor Format tab of the Options dialog box. With this tab, you can customize the way the VBE looks.

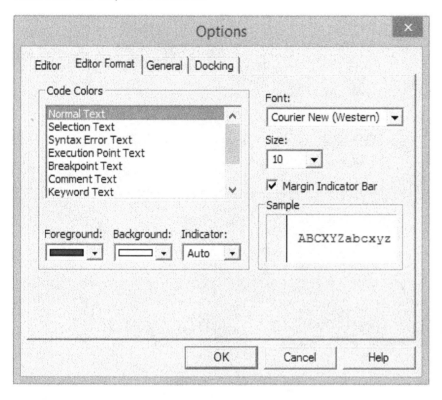

Code Colors: The Code Colors option lets you set the text color and background color displayed for various elements of VBA code. Usually, we don't want to change this setting, default option is ok. But if you like to change the way the code is colored, you can go ahead.

The Font: You can change the font size used in the VBA modules. For best results, stick with a fixed-width font such as Courier New. In a fixed-width font, all characters are the same width. This makes your code more readable because the characters are nicely aligned vertically and you can easily distinguish multiple spaces.

The Size: This is font size in the VBA modules. You can change if you want.

The Margin Indicator Bar: This option controls the display of the vertical margin indicator bar in your modules. You should keep this turned on; otherwise, you won't be able to see the helpful graphical indicators when you're debugging your code.

The General tab

The image shows the options available under the General tab in the Options dialog box.

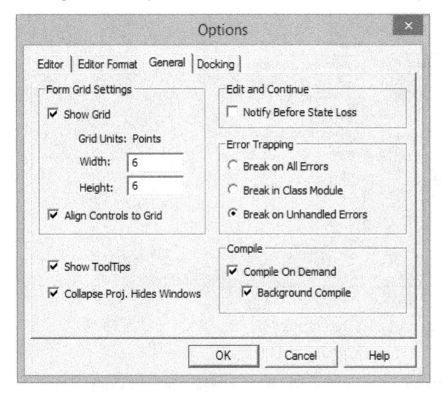

In almost every case, the default settings are ok. The most important setting on the General tab is Error Trapping. If you are just starting your Excel macro writing career, it's best to leave the Error Trapping set to Break on Unhandled Errors. This ensures Excel warns you of errors as you type your code, as opposed to waiting until you try to run your macro.

The Docking tab

The figure shows the Docking tab.

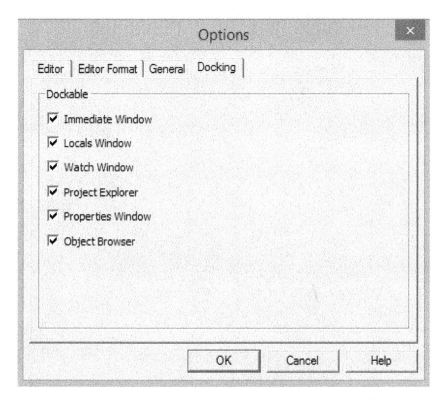

These options determine how the various windows in the VBE behave. When a window is docked, it is fixed in place along one of the edges of the VBE program window. This makes it much easier to identify and locate a particular window. If you turn off all docking, you have a big, confusing mess of windows. Normally, the default settings are ok.

Modules and Codes

In the Project window, you can create so many modules. And in these modules you can put all the macros. You can put the codes inside a single module, or you can put the codes in different modules according to the purpose for which you are using.

Suppose you have made some procedures for Marketing department you can put it in a single module and name the module as Marketing. Like that you can create for Sales department also. Apart from this, you can name the modules according to the behavior. For example, if you are creating various reports for all the departments, then you can create a module by the name Reports.

My personal opinion is you should always name the modules according to the usage or department wise or a combination of both. In this way, it will be easy to maintain the codes.

Modules must have a name for you to identify the Projects quickly and for better maintainability. See the image below.

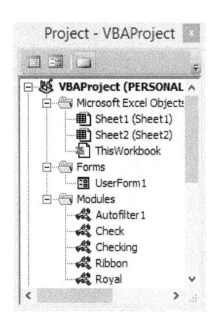

Chapter 4

Excel Object Model, Procedures and Functions

Excel, as I have mentioned earlier is an Object and each object contains other objects arranged in a hierarchical order.

For Example, Excel application contains these Objects

Window, Addin, Worksheets, Workbook, Chart, Sheets, Name, VBProject, Window, Worksheet

Each of these objects has other objects down the line.

So basically you have to manipulate these objects to get your job done with the help of VBA.

Object Hierarchy in Excel

Imagine you want to enter your name in A1 cell on sheet1 you have saved as **Myname.xlsx**. Usually, you will open the Excel file and enter your name in the cell A1.

But if you want to do it using VBA, you should know the objects and how the objects are linked together. In VBA to enter the value in cell A1, you have to write like this.

Application.Workbooks("**Myname.xlsx**").Worksheets("Sheet1").Range("A1"). value = "Name"

Application means the topmost object which is **Excel** itself in Word it is Word and PowerPoint it is PowerPoint.

Workbooks("Myname.xlsx") means the Excel file named **Myname.xlsx**

Worksheets("Sheet1") means the sheet1 of the Excel file **Myname.xlsx**.

Range("A1") means the cell A1 in the Range.

You think this hierarchy is pretty long to just enter a value in cell A1. But if you want to specifically write to the Myname file, then you have to write like this. Otherwise, you can write **Range("A1").value = "Name"**.

Each objects may have many methods and properties. Here if you want to write your name in A1 cell, you have to use the value property of the Range object. So we have used the property value of the Range to write to cell A1.

Here the Application means Excel itself followed by Workbooks object followed by Worksheets then Range object and the value property. Each object is connected with a dot in a hierarchical order. This is called a fully qualified reference; means from top object to bottom everything is covered. You will know just by looking that the Name is in the cell A1 of sheet1 which is saved as Myname.xlsx.

You may skip using the fully qualified reference. In this case, you can skip writing the word Application as you know Excel is the Application. Likewise, you can skip the next two objects Workbooks and Worksheets and can get away with write Range("A1").value = "Name". The problem is if there are so many files opened, VBA will always write the Name to any sheet in the Excel file you have just selected or recently opened. You will not have any control over to which workbook the value will be written.

Now we will go in the reverse order to fully understand this. If you write the code Range("A1"). value = "Name", it will write to the last selected Excel files A1 cell.

If you write the code Worksheets("Sheet1").Range("A1"). value = "Name" it will write to the last opened Excel files A1 cell in sheet1.

If you write the code Workbooks("Myname.xlsx").Worksheets("Sheet1").Range("A1"). value = "Name", then it will only write to Myname.xlsx files A1 cell in Sheet1.

So if you want to be dead sure the value is to be written to a particular file then use fully qualified reference.

If you are still confused don't worry, going forward we will be writing small procedures for you to understand.

Properties and Methods

Almost all the Objects have Properties and Methods of their own. Some properties are read only, means you cannot change the property value, but for some properties you can change. Methods in VBA mean it can do some action on the Object.

For example, all the cell ranges belong to the Range Object and Range has a property called value. If you write **Range("A1").value = 10,** then A1 cell value will become 10.

Also, Range has a method called copy to copy the contents. You can write like this **Range("A1").Copy** to copy the contents of the cell A1. From these two examples, you might have got some idea about properties and methods.

Procedures

In Visual Basic, a set of commands to perform a specific task is placed into a procedure. This can be a Function procedure or a Sub procedure (also known as functions and subroutines). The main difference between a Function and Sub procedure is Function procedure returns a result (just like Sum function in Excel), whereas a Sub procedure does not.

Sub Procedures

Sub is used to write VBA statements or group of instructions which when called will execute as per the order written. Remember the example I have explained before to change the First row to Bold and font to red. This type of instructions can be written using Sub.

Sub procedure will always start with **Sub** and a name (you can give a meaningful name which conveys what the Procedure do) followed by parentheses **()** and ends with **End Sub.** For example, if you want to write a program to display a message, it will be like this.

Sub DisplayMessage ()

Msgbox "This is a message"

End Sub

Some programmers use an underscore in between the procedure name to make it more readable like this **Display_Message.** I use both ways to name the procedure.

You can pass any arguments to this sub by putting the arguments in between the parentheses. For example, you can write a procedure to find out the product of two numbers and can pass the numbers to this procedure like this FindProduct(2,3).

Keep in mind whatever you are recording using the Macro recorder will always be a Sub Procedure.

Points to Note:

Unlike Java, VBA is not case sensitive, so you can write in whatever case you want. You can give a Procedure name like **DuPeReMOve** or **duperemove** VBA doesn't mind, but it is better you follow a standard. You should name the procedure in such a way that by just looking at the procedure name you should know what the procedure is intended for. I usually make the first letter capital and if it is two words combined, I will make the second words first letter also in upper case like this **DupeRemove.** Or else you can put an underscore between the two words like this **Dupe_Remove.** To be frank, I use both the methods as I like.

Function Procedures

A function procedure is a group of VBA statements that do some calculation according to the code you have written and return a single value or an array. For example, the SUM formula is same as Function Procedure. You will input all the cell values or cell reference you want to get the Sum and it will return with a single answer, the sum of all values.

Function procedure will always start with Function and a name (you can give a name which is meaningful to you) followed by parentheses and ends with End Function like this example.

Function CommissionCalc (comm)
CommissionCalc = comm * 20/100
End Function

You may be thinking why you have to create a function as so many functions or formulas are available in Excel. The answer is very simple; your requirement will be different and is not readily available in the existing Excel functions. Just look at the CommissionCalc example we have just created. It will calculate twenty percent of the input you give. You can use it like the regular Excel function or call from another sub procedure.

Points to note:

Always give functions a prefix indicating the data type of their return value to be helpful in understanding code. For example, b for boolean or i for integer (This part of prefixing the data type is explained in detail in the variable declaration section).

When calling a function, always place open and closed parentheses after the function name. This will distinguish it from a variable or subroutine name, even if the function takes no arguments.

Functions will only return value only. We cannot manipulate objects with function you have to write subs for that.

Naming Sub and Function Procedures

You can name your Sub and Function procedures whatever name you want, you can give X, Y or Z, but this is not a good programming practice. Always try to provide a meaningful name which conveys to you what the Sub or Function procedure is doing.

These are rules which you have to remember while giving a name.

You can use letters, numbers, and some punctuation characters, but the first character must be a letter.

You can't use any spaces or periods in the name.

You can't embed any of the following characters in a procedure name: #, $, %, &, @, ^, *, or !.

If you write a Function procedure to use in a formula, avoid using a name that looks like a cell address like B1 or C1 or XFD214.

Procedure names cannot be longer than 255 characters.

Scope of the Sub and Function Procedures

By default scope of the Sub or Function procedure is Public, means any procedure can access and make use of. Procedures declared as private will not appear in the Excel's Insert Function dialogue box. So basically if you mention the word Private before the Procedure name that procedure can be called from that module only. It cannot be called from any other module.

If your VBA code needs to call a function that's defined in another workbook, set up a reference to the other workbook by choosing the Visual Basic Editor (VBE) Tools → References command.

If you have created the function as an add-in file, then you can use the function like any other function in Excel. It will be available in all the Excel files once the add-in is installed.

Chapter 5

Elements of VBA Language

Variables

In Excel, we store the values in cells. You can enter the word **Sam** in cell A1 and the number 25 in cell A2. Like that, for storing the values in VBA, we use variables. We will go through a simple example for you to understand. Open VBE using the keyboard shortcut Alt + F11 or click Visual basic under Developer tab.

Now create a module by right-clicking sheet1 or sheet2 object from the Project Explorer (If Project Explorer is not visible select view > Project Explorer). Now a new module will be created in the name of Module1. Double click Module1 and paste or type this code. Going forward put all the codes under this chapter in this module. If you want you can keep all the codes in this book in a single module. Or else after each chapter you create a new module and store the codes.

Also, keep in mind all the macros which you have typed will be lost if you save it as **.xlsx** extension. For that, you have to save it as macro enabled workbook extension **.xlsm**. As stated earlier this is done by Microsoft to ensure that the person getting the file will understand the Excel book contains macros. You can type all the examples one after the other in this new module created.

You can type this code in sheet1 or sheet2 or sheet3 object's code window. But if you want this program to work on all sheets, you have to put it in a module's code window. Sheet1 or Sheet2 object's code window is specifically for entering codes of those sheets only.

Now we will start with our first example. As stated earlier all these example files can be downloaded from my website ExceltoVBA.com. Right now type this code beginning from Sub to End Sub in the new module.

Example: Chapter 5.1 - VariableExamp.txt

Sub VariableExamp()

FirstValue = "Sam"

SecondValue = 25

Range("A1").Value = FirstValue

Range("A2").Value = SecondValue

End Sub

After typing click Run from the Run menu or click F5 or click the Play icon in the Standard toolbar. You will get the value Sam in A1 cell and 25 in cell A2. We have used two variables FirstValue and SecondValue to store the values. You can use any word for variables. Instead of FirstValue, you can use X or Y or First or whatever name you want. We have stored the text Sam in the variable FirstValue and 25 in the variable SecondValue. After that, the values are added to the cells A1 and A2 using the Range objects value property.

We will go in depth in the coming sections about data types, variable declaration and assigning. You will get a good picture after that. For the time being, you must understand variables are used to store data.

Data Types

Usually, we will declare a variable with a data type. Datatype determines what the variable is going to hold. In Excel, you can change the data format of a cell to Text or General or Date. Like that in VBA, you can determine what each variables datatypes are.

Given below is the list of data types available in VBA. First, one Byte can hold the numbers from 0 to 255, Integer can hold from −32,768 to 32,767. If your calculation is based on row numbers, then Byte or Integer will not hold the row numbers. There are more than ten lakh rows in Excel starting from Excel 2010. Also nowadays the memory is not a problem for modern day computers, so it best to use Long data type instead of Integer.

Given below is the list of data type and the range of values.

Data Type   **Range of Values**

Byte - 0 to 255
Boolean - True or False
Integer - 32,768 to 32,767
Long - 2,147,483,648 to 2,147,483,647
Single - 3.402823E38 to −1.401298E-45 (for negative values), 1.401298E-45 to 3.402823E38 (for positive values)
Double - 1.79769313486232E308 to −4.94065645841247E-324
(negative values); 4.94065645841247E-324 to
1.79769313486232E308 (for positive values)
Currency - 922,337,203,685,477.5808 to 922,337,203,685,477.5807
Date - January 1, 0100 to December 31, 9999
Object - Any object reference
String (variable length) - 0 to approximately 2 billion characters
String(fixed length) - 1 to approximately 65,400 characters
Variant(with numbers) - Any numeric value up to the range of a double data type. It can also hold special values, such as Empty, Error, Nothing, and Null.

Variant(with characters) - 0 to approximately 2 billion

Declaring and assigning the value to the Variable

In Excel, you can format the cell as number or text or data. Likewise in VBA, you can declare the variable as text or number or date according to what is going to store. In VBA text is called String and for the number you can use Integer or Long or Single or Double.

For declaring the variable names, you have to use the keyword **Dim** followed by the variable name and keyword **as** and the data type like this.

Dim MyName As String
Dim YesorNo As Boolean
Dim Age as Integer
Dim RoomTemperature As Double

We will go through the example below to understand the variable declaration and assignment. As mentioned above type these codes in the new module created below the first example.

Example: Chapter 5.2 - VariableTypes.txt

Sub VariableTypes()

Dim MyName As String
Dim YesorNo As Boolean
Dim Age as Integer
Dim RoomTemperature As Double

MyName = "Sam"
YesorNo = False
Age = 30
RoomTemperature = 25.69
VarVariable = 25
VarVariable = "John"
VarVariable = 65.85

End Sub

Here we have declared the variable MyName as String like this **Dim MyName As String.** String datatype is used to store texts and we stored the name Sam in this variable. Second, we have declared the variable **YesorNo** to store True or False (Boolean datatype will be either True or False). Third, we have declared the age as Integer. An integer can hold only whole numbers, means numbers without decimals. And fourth we have declared the variable **RoomTemperature** as double (datatype used to store decimal numbers).

Once the variables are declared, you can assign the values to the variable declared. For assigning a value to a variable VBA uses an equal sign. Here equal means "assigned to" rather than "equal to". Also, it is used as checking condition like if x = 5 (x value is equal to 5), assignment operator like Range("H1").value = 2 to put the value 2 in H1 cell. Here equal sign means we are storing the value to the variable declared. So if you write **MyName = "Sam"** the text Sam is stored in the variable MyName. If you are assigning a string variable, you have to put the value in double quotes to denote it is a String. Likewise, we are assigning the data for each variable in the example.

Here the last variable **VarVariable** is not declared. If you don't assign any data type to the variable, by default the variable will become Variant. This variable will change the data type internally according to the data you are using. Variant will change to text if it is text and if it is number it will change to number. VBA is not a strictly typed language like Java. So you can assign the values without declaring the variable as String or Boolean or Integer. So these types of variable will be treated as Variant.

So here you can see the same variable is holding the number 25 and after that, it holds the text John and then the decimal 65.85.

You can write programs without declaring variables. But you must declare variables as it is easy to fix any bugs later and your program will run much faster.

We will go through another example.

Example: Chapter 5.3 - FindProduct.txt

Sub FindProduct()

Dim FirstValue As Integer
Dim SecondValue As Integer
Dim Answer As Integer

FirstValue = 25
SecondValue = 10
Answer = FirstValue * SecondValue

MsgBox (Answer)
End Sub

This procedure is to find out the product of 25 and 10. For that first, you have to declare two variables, FirstValue and SecondValue. Then we will assign the values 25 and 10 using the equal sign to these two variables. Now if you want to multiply 25 by 10 you can just type **FirstValue * SecondValue** (star sign is used for multiplication in VBA). Variable Answer is used to hold the product of first and second values.

Then we will use the built-in function Msgbox to popup the value 250 stored in Answer variable. For that, you have to put the variable Answer inside the parentheses after typing MsgBox.

If you run this, you will get a MsgBox like this.

Imposing variable declaration with Option Explicit

You can write programs in VBA without declaring variables. But it is good programming practice that you should declare variables. Whatever variables you are using should be declared as Integer or Boolean or the datatype you will feel appropriate. Otherwise, the variables will be automatically converted to Variant type. You should avoid the use of the Variant data type wherever possible. Data stored in a variant can behave unexpectedly and the bugs related to Variant are very very difficult to find out. There are two main benefits for declaring of Variables.

Programs will run faster – Programs will run much faster if you declare the Variables. If VBA knows which data type is declared it can assign that much memory and programs will run faster.

Easy to find out misspelled variables – If you have misspelled the variable names somewhere in the program it will be easy to spot the spelling error. Otherwise, it is very difficult to spot this error.

If you want to force yourself to declare all variable you can put **Option Explicit** at the beginning of the Module. If this statement is present at the beginning of the module, VBA won't execute the procedure and will give the Compile error Variable not defined. You can change the setting in VBE to insert the Option Explicit statement automatically whenever you insert a new VBA module. Enable the Require Variable Declaration option in the Editor in VBE Tools → Options. It is highly recommended you should enable this option. However, this option will not disturb existing modules; only modules created after it is enabled.

Naming the Variables

When you declare the variables always give meaningful names to remember what the variable is going to store. For example, if you are declaring a variable to hold students score, don't declare the variable as X or Y. Instead, use the variable name as Score or Students_Score. If there is only one variable, you can get away with it. But in bigger programs with so many variables it will be confusing to remember what is X or Y.

One more thing can be done to make it even better by adding a datatype the variable is going to hold. We will discuss the same in the next section.

Rules for declaring variables in VBA.

The first character of the variable must be alphabet and the name can be as long as 254 characters. Also, you can use numbers and some punctuation characters. I usually declare the name like this Dim MyName As String, first and the second main word will be in Capital letters. Or you can use like this My_Name (underscore character in the middle of the variable name to make it more readable).

VBA is not case sensitive, so the variable MyName or myname or Myname are all the same.

You can't use spaces or periods or special type declaration characters (#, $, %, &, or !) in a variable name.

Naming convention

You should have a naming convention when you declare variables in procedures. Especially, if you are doing big projects, this will save huge amount of time. This will enable you to debug the program faster and also allow you to understand the program better. By just looking at the variables you will know what datatype the variable is holding.

For example, if you are declaring a long datatype variable for holding row numbers you can name it as LastRow, no one is going to complain. But if you prefix the letter l before the variable name (for long datatype) like this lLastRow then you can instantly recognize the data type it is holding is Long. If you encounter this variable down the line you don't have to scroll up and see whether it is long or integer.

Like this, you can use b for Boolean and i for Integer. You can make your own naming conventions. Usually, programmers use something like this.

i for Integer

b for Boolean

l for long

s for Single

d for Double.

c for Currency

obj for Object

Once you have made the naming convention always stick to that so that in future the programming and debugging will be easy.

Another use of variable declaration is, you can use the shortcut key to fill up the variable name easily. Enter the first few characters of the name and press Ctrl+Spacebar to activate an auto-complete list of all names that begin with those characters. As you type additional characters, the list continues to narrow down. Given below is an example from one of the procedure when you use the shortcut Ctrl+Spacebar after typing the word Firs.

```
Sub test()

Dim LastRow As Long
Dim FirstName As String
Dim FirstRow As String

Firs
```
🔧 FirstName
🔧 FirstRow
🔹 Fix
🔹 Format
🔹 Format$
🔹 FormatCurrency
🔹 FormatDateTime

Scope of a Variable

The scope of the variable means where can we use this variable, mainly it is procedure-wise, module wise and all modules.

Single Procedure or Local variable - By declaring the variable using Dim or Static within the procedure.

Single Module or Module wise - By declaring the variable using Dim or Private before the first procedure in the module.

All Modules - By declaring the variable using Public before the first procedure in a module. Public variables are dangerous. They can be modified anywhere in your application without warning, making their values unpredictable. Always create variables with the minimum scope possible. Begin by creating all your variables with local (procedure level) scope and only widen the scope of a variable when it is necessary. This is explained in detail with an example in the next section.

As with most rules, there are a few cases where the variable scope rule should be broken because the use of public variables is necessary. Procedure wise and Module wise variables are explained in detail in the next section.

Also, there is another thing you should keep in mind. The variable declared should serve one purpose only. We will look into an example for you to understand.

Example: Chapter 5.4 - FindProduct.txt

```
Sub FindProduct()

Dim FirstValue As Integer
Dim SecondValue  As Integer

FirstValue = 25
SecondValue = 10

FirstValue = FirstValue * SecondValue
MsgBox (FirstValue)

End Sub
```

This is the same example we have just gone through to find out the product of 25 and 10. Here we have declared two integer variables FirstValue, SecondValue and assigned 25 and 10 to the variables. Now we found the product by multiplying the two values and assigned to FirstValue and displayed it using the message box function. We didn't declare a third variable to hold the product as in the previous example. Instead, we reused the variable FirstValue to hold the product.

This program will work correctly because there is nothing wrong with the program. But variable FirstValue is reused to store the product of the two numbers. This will cause confusion what the variable FirstValue is used for. Is it for storing First value or Product value?

What you should do is to declare another variable Answer and assign the product to this variable and display it. If it is a small program, you can easily find out that you have reused the FirstValue. But if you are writing big programs with hundreds of line, then it will be difficult to understand the logical structure of the program.

Single Procedure variable or Local Variable

This is the most efficient way to declare the variable. This is done by declaring the variable within the Procedure which starts with **Sub** and **End Sub.** Usually, we declare the variable right after the Procedure name. Once the procedure ends Excel frees up the memory allocated to the variable.

You can have the same variable name within different Procedures as other procedures cannot access the variable declared in the other modules. We will look into the examples given below for you to understand.

Example: Chapter 5.5 - AB.txt

```
Sub A()

Dim LastRow As Integer
Dim a As Interior, b As Integer, c As Integer
```

```
Dim x, y, z As Integer
LastRow = 3

End Sub

Sub B()

Dim LastRow As Integer
LastRow = 25

End Sub
```

In the above procedure **A**, we have declared seven variables. You can declare the variable in a single line like LastRow variable or declare individually in a single line separating each variable with a comma. Also, we have declared three variables x, y, and z, but we have not given the datatype for x and y. These two variables will be converted to Variant datatype. As I have stated earlier this is not a good way to declare a variable, it slows down the program.

The variable LastRow is present in both the modules with different values. Since both are in separate procedures, their scope will not go beyond the procedure. The LastRow value of 3 in first procedure will not get mixed with 25 in the second procedure. In other words, once the First procedure is completed the variables declared within the first procedure will be destroyed along with all the values it holds.

So if you run procedure **B,** LastRow variable will be created again.

If you want the variable to retain its value when the procedure ends you have to declare it as static variable. Here is an example.

Example: Chapter 5.6 - StaticSub.txt

```
Sub StaticSub()

Static Counting As Long
MsgBox Counting
Counting = Counting + 1
MsgBox Counting

End Sub
```

Usually, if the procedure ends the variable value will be destroyed. Here we have declared the **Counting** variable as Static so it will retain the value. Run this Procedure two three times in a row and you can see the variable is retaining the last value when the procedure ends. To display the value I have put two Msgboxes. First one will give the first value stored and the second one will give the value after the addition.

If you close all the Excel sheets, then the value will get lost and will reset to zero.

Remove the word Static and use Dim. Then run the macro two-three times and see what happens. You will get the same result every time.

Single Module or Module wise

In this type, you have to declare the variable at the beginning of the module before any Procedures are written. In this way, this variable will be available in both the Procedures.

Usually, the value of a module-wide variable does not change when a procedure normally ends (that is when it reaches the End Sub or End Function statement). An exception is if the procedure is halted with an End statement all module-wide variables lose their values.

Example: Chapter 5.7 - FirstSecond.txt

```
Dim LastRow As Integer

Sub First()
LastRow = 3
Call Second
End Sub


Sub Second()
Msgbox (LastRow)
End Sub
```

Open a new module and type the above codes. Since we have mentioned the LastRow variable at the beginning of the module, it will be available in both the procedures. So whatever value is assigned to LastRow in the First procedure is available in the Second procedure as well. After assigning the value '3' to LastRow variable in First procedure, we are calling the Second Procedure from First using the statement **Call** and the Procedure name. In the Second Procedure, we are just putting a Msgbox to display the value.

Points to Note:

Call is used to call another procedure. You have to mention Call followed by the procedure name. You can call without mentioning call but I recommend mentioning the word as it is easy to understand the program.

Please keep in mind while declaring the variable, include a prefix in the variable name so that you can easily identify the scope of the variable. If the variable is in all modules you can prefix it with **p** denoting it is Public, **m** for Module-level and procedure-level don't put anything.

For example, if you are declaring a variable as long and is available in all modules. You can declare like this **Dim plLastRow as Long.** If it is a module wise string variable you can name like **msFirstName.**

Object Variables

An object variable is a variable that represents an entire object, such as a range or a worksheet. Object variables are important for two reasons:

They can simplify your code significantly.

They can make your code execute more quickly. If an object variable is declared VBA will execute faster as it knows what object is defined. Or else you can say if there are lesser dots between the objects and methods or properties program will execute faster. For small programs, this may not matter but for bigger programs speed does matter. This will also make your program easy to maintain

Object variables, like normal variables, are declared with the Dim or Public statement. For example, the following statement declares InputArea as a Range object variable:

Dim InputArea As Range

Use the Set keyword to assign an object to the variable like this **Set InputArea = Range("C16:E16")**

Example: Chapter 5.8 - UsingRangeObject.txt

Sub UsingRangeObject()

Dim Rng1 As Range
Dim Rng2 As Range
Dim Rng3 As Range

Set Rng1 = Worksheets("Sheet1").Range("A1")
Set Rng2 = Worksheets("Sheet1").Range("A2")
Set Rng3 = Worksheets("Sheet1").Range("A3")

Rng1 = 150
Rng2 = 100
Rng3 = Rng1 * Rng2

End Sub

Here we have declared three range variables (Rng1, Rng2 and Rng3) using the Dim keyword. Then we assigned the range to each variable using the Set keyword. So Rng1 will linked to A1, Rng2 to A2 and Rng3 to A3 cell. After that, we assigned 150 and 100 to Rng1 and Rng2. Then we multiplied those two ranges and assigned the product to Rng3. Now if you execute this macro, A3 cell will have the product of Rng1 and Rng2, 15000.

Now in the above example, we just gave a vague name to the range variable. But if you add a meaningful name to the range variable, then it will be very easy to understand what each range holds. For example, if a range consists of volume of sales, you can name the range as SalesVolumeRange.

Here we have declared the range Rng1 as **Worksheets("Sheet1").Range("A1")** so you have to type only Rng1 for any number this range occurrence. Also if you want to change the object variable value, you have to change the Range object only at one place where you have defined.

Comments

Comments are simple statements you put inside the VBA code for you to understand what the particular block of VBA code is doing. Comments start with an apostrophe('), whatever begins after the apostrophe will not be executed by the Compiler.

Example: Chapter 5.9 - AddTwo.txt

Sub AddTwo()

Dim First As Integer	' declares first variable to store first number
Dim Second As Integer	' declares second variable to store second number
Dim Result As Integer	' declares third variable to store the result
First = 2	
Second = 4	
Result = First + Second	' first and second variable is added here

MsgBox Result

End Sub

In the above example, we are adding the two numbers 2 and 4 to get the answer 6. For that, we have created two variables to store the two values and the third variable Result is used to hold the sum of First and Second number.

I have commented each variable on the right side using an apostrophe. For simple programs, it is easy to understand the code logic without comments. But if you are writing hundreds of lines of codes, you must comment it heavily to understand the logic of the program. Even if you are an experienced programmer after six months you may not easily understand what logic you have used in your program. So we should use the comments to find out what the program is doing. First, you should use comments after the procedure name to understand what that particular procedure is doing. Then you must use the inline comments as in the example given above.

Points to Note:

In VBE you cannot comment an entire paragraph by mentioning it as a comment like other programming languages. For that, you have to manually put the apostrophe before each line. But here is a quick way to put an apostrophe before each line of code. In the VBE, choose View ⇨Toolbars ⇨ Edit to display the Edit toolbar. This one is very useful when writing the programs to debug as well putting a comment, so make a big note of this. You will get a toolbar like in this image.

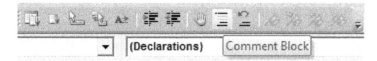

In that, if you click the icon on the right side of the hand icon you can comment out the entire block of code.

If you want to uncomment the entire block, then click the next icon beside the Comment block to uncomment the entire the block or a single line comment.

Always keep in mind that code commenting is one of the most important practices in programming even if you are making a small procedure or Excel application.

These are the three types of comments, Module level, Procedure level and In line comment.

Module level Comment

If you are making a big program, then you should put a comment at the beginning of the module saying what the module contains and written by, or edited by the person's name (if the program is written by a group). If it is a big program, you have to again update the comments once you make the changes in program logic.

Given below is one of the examples you can make use as Procedure level.

```
"=========================================================
" Program     :     UploadSales
" Desc        :     Upload Sales data to the Sales sheet
" Called by    :     SalesPrint
" Call        :     UploadSales weekReport, PrintRow
" Arguments    :     weekReport -- Name of the sales workbook
"                   PrintRow--Number of the row to process
" Comments     :     (1) RunReport initializes the numberRow variable
"

" Changes---------------------------------------------
" Date          Programmer     Change
```

" 8/9/2015   Sam   Written
" 8/10/2016   John   Included a Procedure call MarketingReport to transfer the data to
another Marketing sheet   "==
Sub UploadSales(weekReport, As Workbook, PrintRow As Long)

Procedure level comment

After you declare the procedure name, you should write a comment stating what that particular procedure or function is doing.

In line comment

In line comments are used to give line by line comments to understand the program logic more clearly. For example, if you have a do while loop with do at the beginning of the procedure and while at the end and hundreds of lines of codes in between. In this case, you should make use of the inline comments to better understand the program flow.

Given below is the example of procedure level and In line comments.

Example: Chapter 5.10 – AddTwo.txt

```
Sub AddTwo()

' will add two numbers and display the result in a Message box.

Dim First As Integer          'declares first variable to store the first variable
Dim Second As Integer         ' declares second variable to store the second variable
Dim Result As Integer         ' declares third variable to store the result

First = 2
Second = 4
Result = First + Second       ' first and second variable is added here

MsgBox Result

End Sub
```


Constants Predefined and Declared

Predefined or Built-in Constants.

Excel and VBA make available many predefined constants, which you can use without declaring. In fact, you don't even need to know the value of these constants to use them. The macro recorder usually uses constants rather than actual values. The following procedure uses a built-in constant (xlLandscape) to set the page orientation to landscape for the active sheet.

Example: Chapter 5.11 – ChangeToLandscape.txt

Sub ChangeToLandscape()

   ActiveSheet.PageSetup.Orientation = xlLandscape

End Sub

Also, these constants have a predefined number. So instead of the constant name, you can use these predefined numbers. For example, xlPasteValues is -4163 and xlPasteAll is 4104. But it is better to use the constant name itself instead of the numbers to easily understand what it is.

If you need to know the value of a constant at design time, right-click over the constant name in the VBE and choose definition from the shortcut menu. If it is a built-in constant object browser will open with the details of the constant. If you have defined the constant then you will be brought directly to the line where the constant is defined.

In break mode at runtime, it's even easier. Just hover your mouse over the constant and a ToolTip window containing its value appears.

Declared or your own Constant Values

Sometimes you want to declare some values which don't change, you can declare as constant. For example, if an interest rate of a loan appears so many times in a macro, you can declare the same as constant. Then refer this constant name instead of hardcoded value directly. If the rate changes you are required to change only in one place.

For declaring the constant you can use the keyword **Const** with the data type and the constant value in a line. Here is an example for you to understand.

Example: Chapter 5.12 - ConstantExamp.txt

Sub ConstantExamp()

Dim LoanAmount As Long
Dim InterestPart As Long
Const InterestRate As Integer = 18

LoanAmount = InputBox(" Enter the loan amount")
InterestPart = LoanAmount * InterestRate / 100

MsgBox InterestPart

End Sub

Here we have declared two long variables LoanAmount and InterestPart to hold Loan amount and Interest Amount. Then we have declared an integer constant called InterestRate using the Const keyword.

The loan amount we are getting from the user by using the built in method Inputbox is stored in LaonAmount. Then we are calculating the interest part by multiplying the loan amount with Interest rate. Then this is stored in the variable InterestPart. Then we are displaying the Interest part using the built in method Msgbox.

Points to Note: Please don't try to change the value of the constant down the line once it is declared. It will result in error as constants value cannot be changed.

For example, if you add a line, InterestRate = 20 as the last line of code in the above example, it will result in an error. Try it for yourself.

Obviously, you may think you can use a variable instead of constant. But variable value can be changed accidentally by you or some other person down the line and the final result will change. Another advantage is if any other person changes the interest rate he will get a compile error stating value of the constants cannot be changed. The person who changes will immediately understand this is a constant value and should not be changed. Especially useful if there are more than one programmers.

Arrays

An array is a group of like-typed variables that are referred to by a common name. Arrays of any data type can be created and may have one or more dimensions.

For example, if you want to store thirty student names in VBA, you have to create thirty variables with different names. But if you are declaring it as an array, you can declare a single variable name as an array and can store thirty names with an index number for each student. In VBA array starts at 0 so the first name will have the index number 0 second number will have 1 and so on. These stored names or individual values in the array are called elements of an array. These can be retrieved using the index number we specified.

One Dimensional Array:

This array can be declared like this.

Dim arrayName(index) as dataType

or

Dim arrayName(first index to last index) as dataType

When you declare an array, you need to specify only the upper index, VBA assumes that 0 is the lower index. So if you declare **Dim Month(11) as String** the lower index will be 0. Else if you want to start the index at one, you can declare it like this **Dim Month (1 to 12) as String.**

Example: Chapter 5.13 - Month_Array.txt

Sub Month_Array()

Dim Months(6) As String

Months(0) = "Jan"
Months(1) = "Feb"
Months(2) = "Mar"
Months(3) = "Apr"
Months(4) = "May"
Months(5) = "June"
Months(6) = "July"

MsgBox Months(2)
MsgBox Months(5)

End Sub

Here we have declared the Months variable as array specifying the number of elements by putting 6 in between the parenthesis. So array size will be seven (array starts from 0). Now we have assigned each month to each element of the array starting from index 0 to 6. So index 0 we are holding Jan and in the second index (index(1)) we are holding Feb.

Once you have populated the array with data, you can retrieve the data. For that here we have used Msgbox function mentioning the array name and index number. We will get two message box one after the other with the value Mar and June once you run this macro.

Now if you want the array to start from 1 instead of 0, you have to declare the variable like this.

Dim Months (1 To 7) As String

There is an option to put a VBA statement **Option Base 1** at the beginning of the module to start all the arrays at 1. But it is not recommended as it may not work on other versions of Excel. Instead, always specify both the upper and lower bounds of every array variable you use.

Always keep in mind the array index starts at zero instead of one if you don't specify otherwise. So if you declare an array of ten, it can store eleven elements. Therefore, the two statements that follow have the same effect:

Dim MyArray(10) as String

Dim MyArray (1 to 11) as String

In both cases, the array consists of 11 elements.

Don't hardcode the array index, always use the Ubound and Lbound. If the array index changes in between the program it will be automatically taken care of. You will learn using Ubound and Lbound shortly.

You can also use the Array function in Excel VBA to quickly and easily initialize an array. You will learn that in the VBA array functions in the next section.

Two Dimensional Arrays

Two dimensional arrays can store more items and are the most commonly used ones. This type of array can be declared like this.

Syntax: Dim arrayName (num1, num2) As Datatype, here you can store num1*num2 items

For example, **Dim ArrayFinalData(10,20) as String** can store 10*20=200 items.

This type of array mimics the Excels column and row.

Example: Chapter 5.14 - Month_Array.txt

Sub Month_Array()

Dim Months(2, 3) As String

Months(0, 0) = "Jan"
Months(0, 1) = "Feb"
Months(0, 2) = "Mar"
Months(0, 3) = "Apr"
Months(1, 0) = "May"
Months(1, 1) = "June"
Months(1, 2) = "July"
Months(1, 3) = "Aug"
Months(2, 0) = "Sep"
Months(2, 1) = "Oct"
Months(2, 2) = "Nov"
Months(2, 3) = "Dec"

MsgBox ("Value in Array index 0,3 : " & Months(0, 3))
MsgBox ("Value in Array index 2,1 : " & Months(2, 1))

End Sub

When you execute the above function, it produces the following output.

Value in Array index 0,3 : Apr

Value in Array index 2,1 : Oct

Three Dimensional Arrays

Following is a declaration for a three dimensional array that contains 1,000 elements (visualize this array as a cube):

Dim MyArray(1 To 10, 1 To 10, 1 To 10) As Integer

You can declare up to 60 dimension array in VBA. But in real world, you may not require more than three dimensions as it becomes complicated and difficult to maintain.

Dynamic Arrays

Declaring dynamic arrays

What if you don't know how many elements you want in an array? In this case, you can declare the array dynamically.

For example, today you want to store values of A1:A5 in an array. Tomorrow the values are in A1:A10 and next day it is in A1:A20. In this case, you cannot declare a static array but you have to declare dynamic array as the number of rows changes every day. After that, you can increase or decrease the array size as per your requirement.

A dynamic array is declared with a blank set of parentheses without any elements like this:

Dim MyArray() As Integer

ReDim Statement

ReDim statement is used to declare dynamic-array variables and allocate or reallocate storage space. You can use the ReDim statement any number of times, changing the array's size as often as you need to. If adding a lot of data dynamically do not resize the array after every new element but after every 10 or so. When you change an array's dimensions, the existing values are destroyed. If you want to preserve the existing values, use ReDim Preserve.

Syntax:

ReDim [Preserve] varname(subscripts) [, varname(subscripts)]

Parameter:

First parameter is optional and rest two are required.

preserve – used to preserve the data in an existing array when you change the size of the last dimension.

varname - denotes the name of the variable.

subscripts - indicates the size of the array.

Points to Note: - If you resize an array from bigger to smaller, the data in the eliminated elements will be lost.

In the following example, an array is redefined and the values are preserved when the existing size of the array is changed.

Example: Chapter 5.15 - Array_Preserve.txt

Sub Array_Preserve()

  Dim MyArray() As Variant
  Dim i As Integer

 i = 0

  ReDim MyArray(5)
  MyArray(0) = "PQR"
  MyArray(1) = 35.68
  MyArray(2) = 49

  ReDim Preserve MyArray(7)
  For i = 3 To 7
  MyArray(i) = i
  Next

  'to retrieve the output

  For i = 0 To UBound(MyArray)
    MsgBox MyArray(i)
  Next

End Sub

Here we have declared the array MyArray as variant. Then we used the ReDim to resize the array to five elements. Values PQR, 35.68 and 49 is stored as first three elements. After that we used the ReDim to resize the array to seven along with Preserve to preserve the values you have already stored.

Then we used For loop to populate the remaining part of the array. Once it is filled, we used another For loop to retrieve the values from the array. Here we have used UBound function (explained in the next section).

When you execute the above function, it produces the following output.

PQR
35.68
49
3
4
5
6
7

VBA Array Functions

Array

You can create an array using Array() function with a supplied set of values. You need to provide all the elements required inside Array function and store it in a variable and that variable is converted into array.

Syntax:

Array(Element1, Element2, Element3.....ElementN)

Returns a variant containing an array.

Example: Chapter 5.16 - Array_Func.txt

Sub Array_Func()

Dim Month As Variant
Month = Array("Jan", "Feb", "Mar")
MsgBox Month(1)

End Sub

Three values Jan, Feb and Mar are stored inside Month variable as array because we have used the Array function. Then we displayed the first index value **Feb** using MsgBox function.

Array Methods

There are various inbuilt functions in VBA to handle arrays effectively. These methods are listed below.

LBound

The LBound function returns the smallest index number of the specified array. So if the array index starts from 0 it will give zero and if it is 1 it will give one. Keep in mind we will not get the value stored in array but we will get the smallest index number.

Syntax:

LBound(arrayName[,dimension])

Parameters:

First parameter is required and second one is optional.

arrayName - this is the name of the array.

dimension - An integer value that corresponds to the dimension of the array. If it is '1', then it returns the lower bound of the first dimension; if it is '2', then it returns the lower bound of the second dimension and so on.

Example: Chapter 5.17 - Array_Lbound1.txt

Sub Array_Lbound1()

Dim MyArray(5) As Variant

```
MyArray(0) = "9"          'Number as String
MyArray(1) = "John"       'String
MyArray(2) = 250          'Number
MyArray(3) = 8.95         'Decimal Number
MyArray(4) = #9/20/2016#  'Date
MyArray(5) = #11:32:00 PM# 'Time

MsgBox ("The smallest Subscript value of  the array is : " & LBound(MyArray))
```

End Sub

Here we have declared an array named MyArray as variant of size five. Then we have added each element to the array. First one is **9**, second one is **John**, third one is **250** fourth one is **8.95**, fifth is **#9/20/2016#** and sixth one is **#11:32:00 PM#**.

After that, we have used the LBound function to get the smallest index of the array.

You will get the answer as **The smallest Subscript value of the array is 0.** Here you will get 0 because the array starts at zero where the value **9** is stored. Here we are not referring to the value but where the array starts at, means the index number.

Now we will make a small change to the example and again run this program.

Example: Chapter 5.18 - Array_Lbound2.txt

Sub Array_Lbound2()

  Dim MyArray(2 To 5) As Variant
  MyArray(2) = 250   **'Number**
  MyArray(3) = 8.95   **'Decimal Number**
  MyArray(4) = #9/20/2016# **'Date**
  MyArray(5) = #11:32:00 PM# **'Time**

  MsgBox ("The smallest Subscript value of the array is : " & LBound(MyArray))

End Sub

Now you will get the answer **The smallest Subscript value of the array is 2.** Here we have explicitly declared the array starts at 2.

Now we will look into MultiDimension Array example.

Example: Chapter 5.19 - Array_Multi_Lbound1.txt

Sub Array_Multi_Lbound1()

  Dim MyArray(4, 3) As Variant

  MsgBox ("The smallest subscript of the first dimension of MyArray is : " & LBound(MyArray, 1))
  MsgBox ("The smallest subscript of the Second dimension of MyArray is : " & LBound(MyArray, 2))

End Sub

Here you will get the result as **0** for both the dimension as the array begins at zero for both dimensions.

Example: Chapter 5.20 - Array_Multi_Lbound2.txt

Sub Array_Multi_Lbound2()

  Dim MyArray(2 To 4, 1 To 3) As Variant

  MsgBox ("The smallest Subscript of the first dimension of MyArray is : " & LBound(MyArray, 1))
  MsgBox ("The smallest Subscript of the Second dimension of MyArray is : " & LBound(MyArray, 2))

End Sub

Here you will get the result as

The smallest Subscript of the first dimension of MyArray is : 2

 The smallest Subscript of the Second dimension of MyArray is : 1.

The first dimension of the array we have started at 2 and the second dimension we have started at 1.

Ubound

The UBound Function returns the largest index number of the specified array. Like LBound function, we will not get the value stored in array but the largest index number.

Syntax:

UBound(arrayName[,dimension])

Parameter:

First parameter is required and second one is optional.

arrayName – this is the name of the array.

Dimension - This takes an integer value that corresponds to the dimension of the array. If it is '1', then it returns the upper bound of the first dimension; if it is '2', then it returns the upper bound of the second dimension, and so on.

Example: Chapter 5.21 - Array_Ubound1.txt

Sub Array_Ubound1()

Dim MyArray(5) As Variant

MyArray(0) = "9"   'Number as String
MyArray(1) = "John"   'String
MyArray(2) = 250   'Number
MyArray(3) = 8.95   'Decimal Number
MyArray(4) = #9/20/2016# 'Date
MyArray(5) = #11:32:00 PM# 'Time
MsgBox ("The highest Subscript value of the array is : " & UBound(MyArray))

End Sub

Here we have declared an array named MyArray as variant of size five. Then we have added each element to the array. First one is **9**, second one is **John**, third one is **250** fourth one is **8.95,** fifth is a **#9/20/2016#** and sixth one is **#11:32:00 PM#**.

After that, we have used the UBound function to get the highest index number not the value of the array.

You will get the answer as **The highest Subscript value of the array is : 5**.

Now we will look into MultiDimension Arrays.

Example: Chapter 5.22 - Array_Ubound2.txt

Sub Array_Ubound2()

Dim MyArray(4, 3) As Variant

MsgBox ("The highest subscript of the first dimension of MyArray is : " & UBound(MyArray, 1))
MsgBox ("The highest subscript of the Second dimension of MyArray is : " & UBound(MyArray, 2))

End Sub

Here you will get the result as:

The highest subscript of the first dimension of MyArray is : 4.

The highest subscript of the Second dimension of MyArray is : 3.

First dimension of the array size is 4 and second one is 3, so the highest index number is 4 and 3 for each dimension.

Split

A Split Function returns an array that contains a specific number of splitted values based on a delimiter you provide.

Syntax:

Split(expression[,delimiter[,count[,compare]]])

Parameter:

First parameter is required and rest are optional.

expression - the text you want to split with delimiters.

delimiter -. this is the delimiter based on which we split the text.

count - the number of splitted text to be returned, and if specified as -1, then all the texts are returned.

compare - specifies which comparison method is to be used. Given below are the comparison methods

0 = vbBinaryCompare - Performs a binary comparison

1 = vbTextCompare - Performs a textual comparison

<u>Example: Chapter 5.23 - Array_Split.txt</u>

```
Sub Array_Split()

Dim SalesPerson As Variant
Dim Array_Size As Integer
Dim i As Integer

SalesPerson = Split("John @ Roger @ Donald", "@")
Array_Size = UBound(SalesPerson)

For i = 0 To Array_Size
MsgBox ("The value of array in " & i & " is : " & SalesPerson(i))
Next

End Sub
```

You will get the output like this.

The value of array in 0 is : John

The value of array in 1 is : Roger

The value of array in 2 is : Donald

Here we have declared one variant variable **SalesPerson** and two integer variables ArraySize and i. ArraySize to hold the upperbound of the array and i for For loop. Then we used the Split function followed by the names along with the delimiter @ in double quotes. Second parameter we have given @ so that wherever the @ symbols occurs it will split the names.

Split function will split and return an array of names and this will be stored inside the **SalesPerson** variable. Since the split function returns an array, **SalesPerson** variable will be converted to an array.

We used the UBound function to find out the upperbound of the array which is two (remember array starts at zero).

The we used For Loop to display the values stored in the array.

Join

This function returns a string that contains a specified number of substrings in an array. This is an exact opposite function of Split Method.

Join(list[,delimiter])

Parameter:

First parameter is required and second is optional.

list - an array that contains the substrings that are to be joined.

Delimiter - the character to use as a delimiter. The default delimiter is Space.

Example: Chapter 5.24 - Array_Join.txt

Sub Array_Join()

```
    Dim First As Variant, Second As Variant
    First = Array("Green", "Red", "Blue")
    Second = Join(First)
    MsgBox ("The value of Second is :" & Second)
    Second = Join(First, "$")
    MsgBox ("The Join result after using delimiter is : " & Second)
```

End Sub

Here we declared two variables First and Second as variant. Then we converted the First variable using Array function and stored three values in the array. So First(0) has the value **Green**, First(1) has the value **Red** and First(2) has the value **Blue**.

Then we used the Join function to join all the values of the array and stored in the Second variable. The default value while you use the join function is a single space. So the Second variable will have the value **Green Red Blue.** Now if you want something else instead of space, for example a dollar sign you can give it like this Join(First, "$"). This will store the values like this **GreenRedBlue.**

When you execute the above function, it produces the following output.

The value of Second is : Green Red Blue

The Join result after using delimiter is : GreenRedBlue

Filter

This function searches an array for all the elements that match a given text and returns an array of just the elements that match. If there is no match then an empty array is returned.

Syntax:

Filter(sourcearray, match [,include[,compare]])

Parameter:

First two parameters are required and last two are optional.

Sourcearray – have to specify the one-dimensional array of strings to be searched.

match – specify the string to search against the sourcearray.

Include - this is a Boolean value, which indicates whether or not to return the substrings that include or exclude. If include is False then the non matching values are returned. By default, this is True so you can skip mentioning True.

compare - describes which string comparison method is to be used. Given below are the two methods.

   0 = vbBinaryCompare - Performs a binary comparison

   1 = vbTextCompare - Performs a textual comparison

Example: Chapter 5.25 - ArrayFilterExamp1.txt

```
Sub ArrayFilterExamp1()

Dim a, b, c, d As Variant

a = Array("Red", "Blue", "Yellow")

b = Filter(a, "e")
c = Filter(a, "B")
d = Filter(a, "Y")

MsgBox ("The Filter result b: " & b(0))
MsgBox ("The Filter result c: " & c(0))
MsgBox ("The Filter result d: " & d(0))

End Sub
```

When you execute the above function, it produces the following output.

The Filter result b: Red

The Filter result c: Blue

The Filter result d: Yellow

First we have declared four variables a, b, c and d as variant. Here a, b, c are not declared so it will be variant variable. Then we converted the variable to an array using Array function and stored Red, Blue and Yellow.

Then we used the filter method to filter the elements containing the letter e. Filter method will filter all the elements containing the letter e and store the same as one dimensional array in b variable. Here all the elements have the letter e so all the variables will be stored in b array. So in the first message box the first element of array b is Red.

Second, we filtered out the elements containing the letter B. So only the second element Blue has the letter B. So the first element in the array c will be Blue. There will not be any other element in the array because there is no other word having the letter B.

Like that, letter Y is only in the third element Yellow. So the first element will be Yellow and there will not be any other element in the newly formed array d.

Example: Chapter 5.26 - ArrayFilterExamp2.txt

Sub ArrayFilterExamp2()

Dim a, b, c, d As Variant

a = Array("Red", "Blue", "Yellow")

b = Filter(a, "Y", False)

MsgBox ("The Filter result b: " & b(1))

End Sub

Here we have used the third parameter include as False. So all the elements in the array having the letter Y will be excluded and so in the newly formed array **b**, we have Red and Blue as first and second element. So we will get the answer Blue.

IsArray

This function checks whether the specified input variable is an array variable. You will get Boolean value, True if it is an array and False if not.

Syntax:

IsArray(variablename)

Example: Chapter 5.27 - Isarray_demo.txt

Sub Isarray_demo()

  Dim First, Second As Variant

  First = Array("Green", "Red", "Blue")
  Second = "654789"

  MsgBox ("Is variable First an array: " & IsArray(First))

  MsgBox ("Is variable Second an array: " & IsArray(Second))

End Sub

When you execute the above function, it produces the following output.

Is variable First an array: True

Is variable Second an array: False

Erase

This function is used to reset the values of fixed size arrays and free the memory of the dynamic arrays. It behaves depending upon the type of the arrays.

Syntax:

Erase ArrayName

Fixed numeric array, each element in an array is reset to Zero.

Fixed string array, each element in an array is reset to Zero length " ".

Array of objects, each element in an array is reset to special value Nothing.

Example: Chapter 5.28 - Erase_Examp.txt

```
Sub Erase_Examp()

  Dim NumArray(3) As Variant

  NumArray(0) = "VBA"
  NumArray(1) = 45.09
  NumArray(2) = 65
  NumArray(3) = #9/27/2017#

  Dim DynamicArray() As Variant

  ReDim DynamicArray(10)   ' Allocate storage space.

  Erase NumArray        ' Each element is reinitialized.

  Erase DynamicArray     ' Free memory used by array.

  MsgBox ("The value at Zeroth index of NumArray is " & NumArray(0))

  MsgBox ("The value at First index of NumArray is " & NumArray(1))

  MsgBox ("The value at Second index of NumArray is " & NumArray(2))

  MsgBox ("The value at Third index of NumArray is " & NumArray(3))

End Sub
```

First we created a variant array called **NumArray** of size four and allocated the values to the array. Now we created a **DynamicArray** and allocated a space of ten. Then these two arrays are erased using Erase methods so all the values will be erased.

When you execute the above function, it produces the following output.

The value at Zeroth index of NumArray is

The value at First index of NumArray is

The value at Second index of NumArray is

The value at Third index of NumArray is

Chapter 6

Range Object

Since we are working with Ranges (a group of cells like A1:A10) in Excel, it is vital to understand how we can make use of the Range object. You have to keep in mind there is no Cell object in VBA only Range object. Every procedure you write is someway connected to Range object. So you must have a good grasp of the properties and methods of Range Object.

Range Properties

Range object has so many properties which you can make use of. Given below are some of the main properties we use frequently. In this, some properties are read only and some are read/write properties. For example, Address property is read only as it can only display the cell address, whereas value property can set the value and get the value of a cell.

Value Property

This property can insert values into the cell or cells and also retrieve values from the cell or cells.

The following procedure will insert the value 100 in the cell A1. For that follow these steps.

1. Open an Excel sheet and Click View Macros in Developer Tab and select visual basic to open the VBE. Right click sheet1 or sheet2 object and create a new module. All the examples in this chapter can be stored in this new module.

2. Double click the module you have created to open the code window. Now type the code given below in the code window.

    Sub InsertValue1()

    Range("A1").Value = 100

    End Sub

3. Here Range is the built-in class of VBA which has a property called value. So first we will type the Object name **Range** followed by the cell address you want (cell address should be in bracket

within double quotes) followed by a dot (to call the next hierarchy) and then the property name which is value. After that, we will put the assignment operator = and assign the value 100 to the cell address A1.

In VBA = is used as assignment operator also for assigning values to the cells.

4. Now execute this Macro by clicking the function key **F5,** or clicking the play button while your cursor is inside this macro. Please pay attention if the cursor is in different Procedure, that Procedure will be executed.

Point to Note:

The default property of the Range object is **Value** so you can skip writing the property name and get away with **Range("A1") = 100.** But it is a good programming practice to write the entire property name to make it very clear what property you are using.

If you want to insert the value 100 to a group of cells from A1:A10, change the code like this.

Example: Chapter 6.1 - InsertValue2.txt

Sub InsertValue2()

Range("A1:A10").Value = 100

End Sub

So when you execute this macro all the cells from A1 to A10 will have the value 100.

You will be surprised; within a fraction of a second all the cells are filled.

In the previous examples, we directly called the Range object. If you use only the range object, it will execute the Procedure in the active sheet. But If you want this code executed in a particular Excel sheet, then you have to write the code like this.

Example: Chapter 6.2 - InsertValue3.txt

Sub InsertValue3()

Application.Workbooks("Book2.xlsx").Worksheets("Sheet1").Range("A1:A10").value = 100

End Sub

As explained earlier Application is the Excel Object itself followed by the Workbooks Object which is the collection of all open Workbooks. Then it is followed by all the Worksheets Object and then the Range object and the value property.

The above code will always assign the value 100 to the cells A1 to A10 in the Excel file Book2.xlsx. For this macro to work, you should have a file open in the name of Book2.xlsx.

We will look into some more examples.

In the below example we are writing the values 50 and 100 to the same cell. The result will be 100 in the cell A1. First, we are referring to the Workbook object with the name MyBook.xlsx and going down the hierarchy to Worksheets objects of Sheet1 and referring to the cell A1.

Example: Chapter 6.3 - WriteToCell.txt

Sub WriteToCell ()

Workbooks(" MyBook.xlsx"). Worksheets(" Sheet1"). Range(" A1")   = 50
Workbooks("MyBook.xlsx"). Worksheets(" Sheet1"). Range(" A1")   = 100

End Sub

The first line will write the number 50 in cell A1 and the second line will overwrite it to number 100.

For this program to work, you should open a file with the name MyBook.xlsx.

Now we will look into another example where we are referring to the cell A1 in two different ways. First, we are using the word ThisWorkbook which will always refer to the active Excel sheet. If there are four excel sheets, then it will refer to the Excel sheet which is opened recently or active.

Whereas the second line will always write to A1 Cell, whose workbook name is MyBook.xlsx even if there are two-three Workbooks open.

Example: Chapter 6.4 - WriteToCell1.txt

Sub WriteToCell1 ()

ThisWorkbook.Worksheets(" Sheet1"). Range(" A1") = 50

Workbooks(" MyBook.xlsx"). Worksheets(" Sheet1"). Range(" A1") = 100

End Sub

Points to note:

You should have an Excel file named MyBook.xlsx opened. Otherwise, this code will generate an error.

Here is another example where when you run the below program, you will get a message box with the value stored in cell A1.

Example: Chapter 6.5 - GetCellData.txt

Sub GetCellData()
MsgBox Range("A1").value

End Sub

Before running this procedure, make sure some value is there in the cell A1. Otherwise, you will get a blank Message box.

In this example we we writing the values to the named ranges.

Example: Chapter 6.6 - SetDataNameRange.txt

Sub SetDataNameRange()
Range("Scores").Value = 20
End Sub

For this example to work, first, select some cells (we will use A1:B6) and name the entire cells as **Scores**. For that, select the cells A1:B6 and enter the word Scores in the Name Box (left side of the formula bar where you can see the cell address of the cell). Now if you run this macro, you will get the value 20 in the entire range which you have named as Scores.

Here is another example where we are writing a value to two different ranges.

Example: Chapter 6.7 - NonContiguous.txt

Sub NonContiguous()

Range("A1:A10,B4:B15").value = 20

End Sub

This macro will fill the value 20 in the range A1:A10 and B4:B15.

Cells Property

In the earlier example we have filled the cells A1:A10 using the statement **Range("A1:A10").Value = 100.** Now you can also use the cells property to fill the range like this.

Range(Cells(1, 1), Cells(10, 1)).Value = 100

Here Cells(1,1) means A1, first row and first column. Cells (10,1) means A10, tenth row and first column. In effect we are writing **Range("A1:A10").value = 100**

As you can see cells property is little difficult to write compared to directly referring the cell address like this **Range("A1:A10").** But the advantage of Cells property is we can dynamically populate the cells using loops (Loops are controlled statement which can be executed the number of times we specify. We will learn about loops shortly).

We will go through the below example for you to understand.

Example: Chapter 6.8 - CellsCheck.txt

```
Sub CellsCheck()

Dim i As Integer
Dim InputValue As Integer

InputValue = 100

For i = 1 To 10
Range(Cells(i, 1), Cells(i, 1)).Value = InputValue
InputValue = InputValue + 1

Next i

End Sub
```

First, we have declared two variables, i and InputValue as an integer. And then we used For loop ten times. Each time the loop is run, the i value will increase by one and the cells row number will change each time the loop runs. The value stored in the InputValue will automatically assigned to the cells.

Next line we have given InputValue = InputValue + 1, means each time the loop runs the value stored in InputValue will be increased by 1. So you will get the values 100 to 109 in the cells A1:A10.

Text Property

Text property is a read-only property. For example, if cell A1 contains the value 18.23 and is formatted to display two decimals and a dollar sign ($18.23), then when you execute the code it will display with the format $18.23. But the value property we have just gone through will return only the value omitting the formatting.

Open an Excel sheet and enter 18.23 in A1 cell and format the same as dollar (Change the Accounting number format to dollar or click the $ sign under Home tab).

Example: Chapter 6.9 - TextProperty.txt

```
Sub TextProperty()
   MsgBox Range("A1").Value
   MsgBox Range("A1").Text
End Sub
```

Execute this Macro and you will get two Message box one after the other. The first one with the value as we have used value property and the second one including the formatting in dollar as we have used text property.

MsgBox is built-in function for displaying Message box, will learn more about Msg box function later.

Text property always returns a string and this property is read-only. But in value property, you can get the value or change the cell value.

Offset property

This property will offset or jump the number of rows and columns away from the cell you are currently in. For example, if you are in A1 cell and if you offset one row and column, cell B2 will be selected. You will understand clearly once you run the example given below.

Example: Chapter 6.10 - Offset1.txt

Sub Offset1 ()

Range("A1"). Offset(RowOffSet:=1, ColumnOffset:=1).Select

End Sub

Offset has two parameters RowOffset and ColumnOffset. Since we have mentioned 1 for RowOffset and ColumnOffset it will select the next row and column after the cell A1. We will jump to B2 cell.

Named Parameters

Named parameters are useful so that you can skip adding commas. Here in the above example we have used the parameter name a colon and an equal sign like this **RowOffSet:=1**. This is called named parameters. Using named parameters makes your code more readable and you will know what parameters are passed on. For example, SaveAs method has so many optional arguments. So if you want to save a file, you have to code like this, ActiveWorkbook.SaveAs "D:\MyFile.xls", , , , , True, , , True.

As you can see, there are so many commas in between the arguments. These are the arguments we are not using in the order it is defined in VBA. If you are not using the arguments, you have to leave it blank and put the comma for the next argument. So if there are ten optional arguments, then we have to separate each argument with commas in the order defined in the VBA. You cannot skip the arguments.

But if you mention the arguments using named parameters, you can write the code like this, ActiveWorkbook.SaveAs FileName:="D:\ MyFile.xls", CreateBackup:=True, AddToMru:=True. And the beauty of the named parameters is you can write in any order and the nonused parameters can be completely avoided.

Now we made the procedure shorter by mentioning row and column number directly.

Example: Chapter 6.11 - Offset2.txt

Sub Offset2 ()

Range("A1").Offset(1, 1).Select

End Sub

Now we will look into another example where we are using the cell A1 to B1. From these cells, we are offsetting one row and one column. Once you run this procedure, the cells B2 to C2 will be selected. Since we are offsetting from two cells, the same two cells will get selected from B2.

Example: Chapter 6.12 - Offset3.txt

Sub Offset3()

Range("A1:B1").Offset(1, 1).Activate

End Sub

How to Offset Only Rows?

Example: Chapter 6.13 - OffsetRow.txt

Sub OffsetRow()

Range("B1").Offset(1).Select

End Sub

Here I have omitted the column parameter and its comma. This code results in moving one row down from the original cell location.

How to Offset only Columns?

Similarly, it's possible just to specify the columns and omit the rows. The code will look like this.

Example: Chapter 6.14 - OffsetColumn.txt

Sub OffsetColumn()

Range("B1").Offset(, 1).Select

End Sub

The comma is necessary for Excel to know that only column offset has been set.

How to Specify Negative OffSet?

You can do a negative offset also. We will look into an example.

Example: Chapter 6.15 - OffsetNegative.txt

Sub OffsetNegative()

Range("E2").Offset(-1, -1).Select

End Sub

This makes the selection go up one row and one column from the starting position, from cell E2 we move up to cell D1.

How to OffSet a Range of Cells

Instead of offsetting single cells you can offset a Range. We will go through an example.

Example: Chapter 6.16 - OffseRange.txt

Sub OffseRange()

Range("A1:C4").Offset(1, 1).Select

End Sub

Here, we start off with the range of cells from A1 to C4. The objective is to offset this complete range of cells by 1 row and 1 column and select the new Range. The new range of cells will be from B2:D5.

Using Active Cell with Offset

The active cell refers to the currently selected cell. We will look into this example to understand. This procedure will select one cell down the active cell.

Example: Chapter 6.17 - ActiveCellOffset.txt

Sub ActiveCellOffset()

ActiveCell.Offset(1, 0).Select

End Sub

If you run this program, again and again, it will jump to next cell one by one. By offsetting using ActiveCell, you can dynamically select the cells and is very useful when programming.

For example, you can write a program to copy the adjacent cells if the active cell value is five.

Combining Active Cell with Range() and Offset()

The following code selects a cell in addition to four more to the right which is to be copied /pasted in another location.

Example: Chapter 6.18 - ActiveCellOffsetCopy.txt

Sub ActiveCellOffsetCopy()

Range(ActiveCell,ActiveCell.Offset(0,4)).Copy

End Sub

Take note that there is a comma after the first ActiveCell instance and a double closing parenthesis before the Copy. If you want you can provide the destination cells to copy.

Count property

This property returns the number of cells in a range irrespective of whether cells have any values in it. In other words, it counts the blank cells also in the range. This is a read only property.

Example: Chapter 6.19 - CountProperty.txt

```
Sub CountProperty()
MsgBox Range("A1:C3").Count
End Sub
```

This macro will give the answer 9 as there are nine cells in the Range (including blank or non-blank cells).

Column and Row properties

The Column property returns the column number of a single-cell range; the Row property returns the row number of a single-cell range.

Example: Chapter 6.20 - ColandRow.txt

```
Sub ColandRow()
  MsgBox Worksheets("Sheet1").Range("G3").Column
  MsgBox Worksheets("Sheet1").Range("G3").Row
End Sub
```

You will get two message boxes with 7 in the first box and 3 in the second. G is column number 7 and 3 is row number 3.

If the Range object consists of more than one cell, the Column property returns the first column number and Row property returns the first row number. For example, if we rewrite the above example like this **MsgBox Worksheets("Sheet1").Range("G3:H3").Column** and **MsgBox Worksheets("Sheet1").Range("G3:G6").Row,** it will still give the answer 7 and 3.

Rows and Columns

Rows

The Rows property gives access to a specific row of a range.

Example: Chapter 6.21 - Row_Examp1.txt

Sub Row_Examp1()

Rows(3).Select

End Sub

If you execute this procedure, the entire third row will get selected for the active sheet. And if you want to select the row from two to five, you can rewrite the code to **Rows("2:5").Select.**

This example deletes row four on Sheet1.

Example: Chapter 6.22 - Row_Examp2.txt

Sub Row_Examp2()

Worksheets("Sheet1").Rows(4).Delete

End Sub

The following example will delete all the rows between 1 to 10 which has an even number in the first Column. Before executing this macro enter 1 to 10 in the cells A1:A10.

Example: Chapter 6.23 - DeleteRowEvenNumbers.txt

Sub DeleteRowEvenNumbers()

Dim iRow As Integer

iRow = 10

Do While iRow >= 1
If Cells(iRow, 1) Mod 2 = 0 Then Rows(iRow).Delete
iRow = iRow - 1

Loop

End Sub

Here we have declared an Integer value iRow and assigned the value 10 (we only want to look the rows till 10). Then we have put a Do while loop to count backward from row 10 to 1. We will learn this loop shortly.

In between, we have put an IF condition to check the row number is even. To find out the row number is even we have used Mod function. Mod function will check the reminder of the row number divided by specified number 2 mentioned beside Mod. If the reminder is 0, then the row is even and IF function will delete the row.

Columns

The Columns property gives access to a specific column of a range.

Example: Chapter 6.24 - Column_Examp.txt

Sub Column_Examp()

Columns(3).Select

End Sub

If you execute this procedure, the entire third column will get selected.

And if you want to select the column from two to five, you can rewrite the code to **Columns("2:5").Select.**

Points to Note:

Be careful not to mix up the Rows and Columns properties with the Row and Column properties. The Rows and Columns properties return a Range object. The Row and Column properties return a single value, the row number and column number.

Address property

This one is a read-only property, displays the cell address for a Range object in absolute notation.

The following statement displays $A$1:$E$5 in the message box:

MsgBox Range(Cells(1, 1), Cells(5, 5)).Address

Syntax:

Range.Address([RowAbsolute], [ColumnAbsolute], [ReferenceStyle], [External], [RelativeTo])

Parameters:

All these parameters are optional.

RowAbsolute - Default value is True, returns the row reference as an absolute reference.

ColumnAbsolute - Default value is True, returns the column reference as an absolute reference.

ReferenceStyle - xlA1 (default) returns an A1-style reference. Use xlR1C1 to return an R1C1 reference.

External - False (default) returns a local reference, without including a workbook and worksheet reference.

RelativeTo - The Range object that defines the starting point for a relative range. Use this argument if RowAbsolute and ColumnAbsolute are False, and ReferenceStyle is R1C1.

The following statement displays **A1** in the message box without the dollar sign.

MsgBox Cells(1, 1).Address(RowAbsolute:=False, ColumnAbsolute:=False)

HasFormula property

This property (read-only) returns True if the single-cell Range object contains a formula. Otherwise, it returns False.

If the range consists of more than one cell, VBA returns True only if all cells in the range contain a formula, or False if all cells in the range don't have a formula. The property returns a Null if there is a mixture of formulas and non-formulas.

Be careful with the type of variables you use to maintain the results returned by the HasFormula property. When working with any property that returns a Null, it is easy to generate errors by using the wrong data type.

For example, assume that cell A1 contains a value and cell A2 contains a formula. The following statements generate an error because the range doesn't consist of all formulas or non-formulas and in turn return null.

Dim FormulaTest As Boolean

FormulaTest = Range("A1:A2").HasFormula

To fix this type of situation, you should declare the FormulaTest variable as Variant rather than Boolean, as shown below:

Dim FormulaTest As Variant

FormulaTest = Range("A1:A2").HasFormula

If TypeName(FormulaTest) = "Null" Then MsgBox "Mixed!"

Here the IF condition is checking the returned value is Null and then giving the Msg box with the text Mixed.

Formula property

The Formula property represents the formula in a cell. This is a read-write property, so you can access it to insert a formula into a cell. For example, the following statement enters a SUM formula into cell A13.

Example: Chapter 6.25 - RangeFormula.txt

Sub RangeFormula()

Range("A13").Formula = "=SUM(A1:A12)"

End Sub

Notice that the formula is a text string and is enclosed in quotation marks.

You can retrieve the formula written on the cell like this. Before executing this macro, enter any formula in the cell A1. You can enter =A2 + B2 or simply = 5+9.

Example: Chapter 6.26 - RangeFormula1.txt

Sub RangeFormula1()

Dim Form As String

Form = Range("A1").Formula

MsgBox Form

End Sub

If you are using this property to determine the formula in a cell and the cell doesn't have a formula, this returns the cell's Value property.

NumberFormat property

This property represents the number format (expressed as a text string) of the Range object.

It is a read-write property so your VBA code can change the number format of a cell.

For example, the following statement changes the number format of column A to percent with two decimal places:

Columns("A:A").NumberFormat = "0.00%"

This statement will change the number format having two decimals in the cell A1,
Range("A1").NumberFormat = "0.00".

This statement will change the number format without decimals in the cell A1,
Range("A1").NumberFormat = "0"

Follow these steps to see a list of other number formats. Open an Excel and access the Format Cells dialog box by pressing right clicking the cell or from the Home tab. Select the Custom category to view some additional number format strings.

End Property

Returns a range object that represents the cell at the end of the region that contains the source range. Equivalent to pressing END+UP ARROW, END+DOWN ARROW, END+LEFT ARROW, or END+RIGHT ARROW.

Syntax:

expression.End(direction)

expression - a variable that represents a Range object.

Parameters:

direction - Required XlDirection The direction in which to move.

This statement will select the cell at the top of B column which is B1.

Range("B4").End(xlUp).Select

This one selects the cell at the end of row 4.

Range("B4").End(xlToRight).Select

xlUp and **xlToRight** are constants in Excel.

This statement extends the selection from cell B4 to the last cell in row four that contains data.

Range("B4", Range("B4").End(xlToRight)).Select

FONT.BOLD, UNDERLINE or ITALIC Properties

A Range object's Font property returns a Font object and has many properties. To change some aspect of a range's font, you must first access the range's Font object and then manipulate the properties of that object.

The following expression returns a Font object for a range:

Range("A1").Font

The following statement sets to True the Bold property of the Font object contained in the Range object. This changes the cell value to bold.

Range("A1").Font.Bold = True

This one will underline the values in A1 cell.

Range("A1").Font.Underline = True

This will change the font color of the A1 cell to green.

Range("A1").Font.Color = RGB(0, 255, 0)

This one will change the value in A1 cell to italic.

Range("A1").Font.Italic = True

This one increases the font size of A1 cell to 18.

Range("A1").Font.Size = "18"

This one will strike through the value in A1.

Range("A1").Font.Strikethrough = True

This will subscript the value in A1 cell.

Range("A1").Font.Subscript = True

This will Superscript the value in A1 cell.

Range("A1").Font. Superscript= True

Interior property

A Range object's Interior property returns an Interior object.

For example, the following statement set the ColorIndex property of the Interior object to 3 contained in the Range object:

Range("A1").Interior.ColorIndex = 3

This changes the cell's background color to red.

The ColorIndex values resemble the color palette in Excel and take on any value from 1 to 56. Change the value from 1 to see and see the color changes.

If you need to use standard colors, use the Color property instead of the ColorIndex along with a built-in constant: vbBlack, vbRed, vbGreen, vbYellow, vbBlue, vbMagenta, vbCyan, or vbWhite. For example, the following statement makes cell A1 yellow.

Range("A1").Interior.Color = vbYellow

Name Property

By using the name property, you can name the individual cells or the range. Given below is an example.

Example: Chapter 6.27 - NameCells.txt

Sub NameCells()

Range("A1").Name = "First"
Range("B:B").Name = "Second"

End Sub

Here we have given the name **First** to the cell A1 and **Second** to the entire column B.

Path and FullName

The Path property in Excel VBA returns the complete, saved path to the workbook (Excel file). The FullName property in Excel VBA returns the complete, saved path, including the name of the workbook.

Example: Chapter 6.28 - PathandFullname.txt

Open an Excel file and save it as Path.xls on your desktop.

Sub PathandFullname()

MsgBox Workbooks("Sales.xlsx").Path

MsgBox ActiveWorkbook.FullName

End Sub

Now run this macro. First Message box will provide you the path and second message box will provide you the path along with the file name.

You should have a file name opened in the name of Sales.xlsx for this macro to work.

CurrentRegion Property

CurrentRegion returns a range object representing a set of contiguous data. For example, in the image given below, there is data from cells A1 to B6.

	A	B
1	Name	Amount
2	Sam	10
3	John	65
4	Maya	78
5	Rose	95
6	Jeni	87

Suppose if you want to select the entire range from A1 cell you can write a macro like this.

Example: Chapter 6.29 - Current_Region1.txt

Sub Current_Region1()

Range("A1").CurrentRegion.Select

End Sub

This macro will always select the cells from A1 to till the cell contains the data. If there are any blank Rows and Columns in between, selection will stop just before the blank rows and columns like in the figure given below.

	A	B	C	D
1	Name	Amount		Region
2	Sam	10		South
3	John	65		North
4	Maya	78		East
5	Rose	95		West
6	Jeni	87		South
7				
8	Alan	55		South
9	Ronald	65		North
10	Micky	75		East
11	Laila	85		West
12	Roger	25		South

The beauty of current region property is you don't have to worry about the size of the range. This is very useful if you have written a macro to copy the data and data size changes every day.

For example, first day the data is from A1 to B6 and on second day it is from A1 to B20. Now if you are using the above macro, it will select the entire data irrespective of the size.

Current region property can be clubbed along with Autofilter method to filter the data like the example given below. If you use current region with auto filter, you don't have to specify the range of the auto filter (if the range changes every day). Otherwise, you have to specify the range in Auto filter options.

Example: Chapter 6.30 - Current_Region1.txt

Sub Current_Region1()

Range("A1").CurrentRegion.AutoFilter

End Sub

This macro will turn on Excels filter mode as you can see in the image below. Same like clicking Filter under Data tab.

	A	B
1	Name ▼	Amount ▼
2	Sam	10
3	Jenni	20
4	John	30
5	Loyd	40
6	Mary	50

The Autofilter method is explained later in the chapter.

WrapText Property

This property sets or confirms whether the cell is wrapped. This property returns True if text is wrapped and false if not or Null if the specified range contains wrapped and non wrapped cells.

Excel will adjust the row automatically if the text is lengthy.

Enter the text **Learning Excel is fun** in cell A1 and run this macro.

Example: Chapter 6.31 - WrapTextExamp.txt

Sub WrapTextExamp()

Range("A1").WrapText = True

End Sub

This will wrap the text inside cell A1 and the cell height will be adjusted accordingly.

Example: Chapter 6.32 – WrapTextExamp1.txt

Sub WrapTextExamp1()

If Range("A1").WrapText = True Then

MsgBox "Cell A1 is wrapped"

End If

End Sub

After running the previous macro if you run this macro, you will get the answer as **Cell A1 is wrapped**. WrapText properties checks whether the A1 cell is wrapped or not using IF condition. If it is true it will call the Msgbox function.

ShrinkToFit Property

This property shrinks or confirms whether the cell is shrunk. This property returns True if shrinks to fit in the column width, or Null if this property isn't set to the same value for all cells in the specified range.

Example: Chapter 6.33 - ShrinkExamp.txt

Sub ShrinkExamp()

Range("A1").ShrinkToFit = True

End Sub

This will the shrink the text inside cell A1.

<u>Example: Chapter 6.34 – ShrinkExamp1.txt</u>

Sub ShrinkExamp1()

If Range("A1").ShrinkToFit = True Then

MsgBox "Cell A1 is Shrinked"

End If

End Sub

After running the previous macro if you run this macro, you will get the answer as **Cell A1 is Shrinked**. This property checks whether the A1 cell is shrunk or not using IF condition. If it is true it will call the Msgbox function.

Methods

Methods are used to perform actions in VBA. For example, copy and cut is a method of Range object in Excel. We will go through some of the important methods.

Copy Method

Copying and Pasting.

Now we will learn how to copy and paste using VBA. Please follow the steps given below.

Open a fresh Excel file and enter the value 100 in the cell A1 and record the Macro in absolute mode. Copy the value 100 in A1 to C1 and then stop recording. You will get a code something like this. I have given the Macro name as Copy.

<u>Example: Chapter 6.35 - Copy.txt</u>

```
Sub Copy()
    Range("A1").Select
    Selection.Copy
    Range("C1").Select
    ActiveSheet.Paste
```

End Sub

Range Objects has a method called **Select**; macro recorder is using that method. This method will select the value in cell A1 and will copy the selection using the **Copy** method of the Range. Selection refers to the current selection here we have selected a cell, so this will return a Range Object. Selection is actually a property of Application Object and returns a range Object. We are using the shortcut Selection.copy instead of Application. Selection.Copy. Because Excel is the application, you can skip writing the word Application.

Once it is copied again, the recorder will select C1 cell using **Select** method and paste it using the **Paste** method by using the Active sheet property of the Application object which returns the Range Object. You can write the fully qualified name like this **Application.ActiveSheet.Paste**

Ok now we have gone through the code we got from the Macro Recorder.

Actually we don't have to select the object to copy the object. You can rewrite the entire code in a single line like this.

Example: Chapter 6.36 - Copy1.txt

```
Sub Copy1()
Range("A1").Copy Range("C1")
End Sub
```

Here the Copy method has a destination argument which you can specify as Range("C1") and no need to call the Paste method, as simple as that. This is much faster than copying and pasting because it bypasses the Clipboard and directly paste it to the destination range instead of storing in clipboard and then pasting.

Example: Chapter 6.37 - Copy2.txt

```
Sub Copy2()

Range("A1").Copy Destination:=Range("C1")

End Sub
```

Here we have added the named parameter **Destination** to make it very clear the destination should be C1 cell.

In the below example we want to copy A1 cell value from sheet2 of Excel file **Sam** to cell C1 of sheet3 in the Excel file **John**. In this case, you have to fully write the Object reference from almost the top of Object Hierarchy so that it will always copy the cell A1 from the file Sam to John.

Example: Chapter 6.38 - RangeCopy.txt

```
Sub RangeCopy()
   Workbooks("Sam.xlsx").Sheets("Sheet2").Range("A1").Copy _
     Workbooks("John.xlsx").Sheets("Sheet3").Range("C1")
End Sub
```

Here you cannot use the Range object like this **Range("A1").Copy Range("C1")** or
Sheets("Sheet2").Range("A1").Copy Sheets("Sheet3").Range("C1") because other Excel sheets may
have opened and Macro will get executed in the currently active sheet. So to avoid that we are using the
full name qualifiers including the file name.

Points to Note:

I have used space and underscore (_)at the end of the first line. What this means is Copy argument is
continuing in the second line. You can write the code without space and underscore in a single line. But
for the sake of readability, we are breaking the code to next line by putting the space and underscore (
_).

Please keep in mind this program will not work unless you have the two file names, **Sam** and **John**
opened. Also if you don't have sheet2 in Sam, you have to insert it and Sheet3 should be there in John.
And put a value in A1 cell of Sam for copying.

Till now we have copied only single cells, but we can copy multiple cells also. Given below is an example
of that.

Example: Chapter 6.39 - RangeCopy1.txt
```
Sub RangeCopy1()
Range("A1:C200").Copy Range("D1")
End Sub
```

Here we are providing the range of cells **A1:C200** in the Range object and only providing the destination
cell D1 where you want to copy. It is not required to give the destination cell Range. You have to give
only the first cell and Excel will paste the rest of the cells automatically.

I can rewrite the program with named argument **Destination** to make it clear where it is getting copied.
Please find an example.

Example: Chapter 6.40 - RangeCopy2.txt
```
Sub RangeCopy2()
 Range("A1:C200").Copy Destination:=Range("D1")
End Sub
```

Also, you can do the copying by making the object variables to represent the ranges as shown below. Open the files Sam and John and run this macro. There should be sheet2 in Sam and Sheet3 in John.

Example: Chapter 6.41 - RangeCopy3.txt

```
Sub RangeCopy3()
Dim First As Range, Second As Range
Set First = Workbooks("Sam.xlsx").Sheets("Sheet2").Range("A1")
Set Second = Workbooks("John.xlsx").Sheets("Sheet3").Range("C1")
First.Copy Second
End Sub
```

First, we have declared two object variables First and Second as Range. Then we assigned the range using the Set keyword to First and Second. Once the range is assigned you can copy using the copy method. The beauty of this is if you want to use this range in some other place you can use the Object variable instead of the whole line of code.

Cut Method

Cut and Pasting.

Cut and Pasting a cell is very similar to copying the cell only thing is you have to change the method to **Cut**.

Example: Chapter 6.42 - CutandPaste.txt

```
Sub CutandPaste()
  Range("A1").Cut Range("C1")
End Sub
```

Now if you want to cut and paste a Range, you can change the code to look like this.

Example: Chapter 6.43 - CutandPaste1.txt

```
Sub CutandPaste1()
Range("A1:C200").Cut Range("D1")
End Sub
```

Select method

An important method of the Range object is the Select method. The Select method selects a range.

Example: Chapter 6.44 - RangeSelect.txt

Sub RangeSelect()

Range("A1:B20").Select

End Sub

To select a cell or a range of cells, use the Select method. To make a single cell the active cell, you can use **Activate** method instead of Select.

Clear method

To clear the content of an Excel range, you can use the Clear. This will clear the contents including the formats.

Example: Chapter 6.45 - ClearMethod.txt

Sub ClearMethod()

Range("A1").Clear

End Sub

ClearContents method

Clearcontent will clear only the content of the cell it will leave all the formats as it is.

Example: Chapter 6.46 - ClearContentsMethod.txt

Sub ClearContentsMethod()

Range("A1").ClearContents

End Sub

Delete method

This method deletes the object.

Syntax:

Delete(Shift)

Used only with Range objects. Specifies how to shift cells to replace deleted cells. Can be one of the following XlDeleteShiftDirection constants: xlShiftToLeft or xlShiftUp. If this argument is omitted, Microsoft Excel decides based on the shape of the range.

Delete with shift xlToLeft

Here we are deleting the range A2:C5 and shifting the cells left side. So whatever contents in the cells from D2:D5 including the data on the right side of D2:D5 is shifted to A column.

Example: Chapter 6.47 - Delete_Examp1.txt

Sub Delete_Examp1()

Range("A2:C5 ").Delete Shift:=xlToLeft

End Sub

Image before executing the macro.

	A	B	C	D	E	F	G
1	A	B	C	D	E	F	G
2	A	B	C	D	E	F	G
3	A	B	C	D	E	F	G
4	A	B	C	D	E	F	G
5	A	B	C	D	E	F	G
6	A	B	C	D	E	F	G
7	A	B	C	D	E	F	G

After Executing the macro

	A	B	C	D	E	F	G
1	A	B	C	D	E	F	G
2	D	E	F	G			
3	D	E	F	G			
4	D	E	F	G			
5	D	E	F	G			
6	A	B	C	D	E	F	G
7	A	B	C	D	E	F	G

Delete with shift xlToUp

Here we are deleting the range A2:C5 and shifting the cells up.

Example: Chapter 6.48 - Delete_Examp2.txt

Sub Delete_Examp2()

Range("A2:C5").Delete Shift:=xlUp

End Sub

Image before executing the macro.

◢	A	B	C	D	E	F	G
1	A	B	C	D	E	F	G
2	A	B	C	D	E	F	G
3	A	B	C	D	E	F	G
4	A	B	C	D	E	F	G
5	A	B	C	D	E	F	G
6	A	B	C	D	E	F	G
7	A	B	C	D	E	F	G

After Executing the macro

◢	A	B	C	D	E	F	G
1	A	B	C	D	E	F	G
2	A	B	C	D	E	F	G
3	A	B	C	D	E	F	G
4				D	E	F	G
5				D	E	F	G
6				D	E	F	G
7				D	E	F	G

Delete Range in EntireRow

Here we are deleting the entire rows of the range A2:C10, i.e., rows 2 to 10.

Example: Chapter 6.49 - Delete _ Examp3.txt

Sub Delete_Examp3()

Range("A2:C10").EntireRow.Delete

End Sub

Range object has a property called **EntireRow** which return the entire row. So all the rows from two to ten will be deleted.

Delete Range EntireColumn

Here we are deleting the entire columns of the range "A2:C10", i.e., deleting columns 'A' to 'C'. Range object has a property called **EntireColumn** which return the entire column.

Example: Chapter 6.50 - Delete_Examp4.txt

Sub Delete_Examp4()

Range("A2:C10").EntireColumn.Delete

End Sub

Autofill Method

In Excel, you can auto fill the data from the top cell to the bottom till the row where the data is on the left column. For that, you can select fill from the Home tab. You can fill up, down or a series like 1, 2, 3, etc.

In VBA we can achieve the same with Autofill method. It automatically fills in the cells in a specified destination range based on the specified source range.

Syntax:

range.AutoFill(Destination, [Type])

Parameters:

First parameter is mandatory and second parameter is optional.

destination - The cells to be filled, including the source range.

Type - default value is xlFillDefault, which attempts to select the most appropriate fill type based on the source range. You can also explicitly specify the type using one of the following constants: xlFillDays, xlFillFormats, xlFillSeries, xlFillWeekdays, xlGrowthTrend, xlFillCopy, xlFillMonths, xlFillValues, xlFillYears, xlLinearTrend.

In the below example, we are filling the series from 1 to 10 in A1:A10.

Example: Chapter 6.51 - Autofill_Examp1.txt

Sub Autofill_Examp1()

Range("A1") = 1
Range("A1").AutoFill Destination:=Range("A1:A10"), Type:=xlFillSeries

End Sub

First, enter the value 1 in A1 cell. Then we give the data Range("A1") used for autofilling followed by the Destination we want to fill the data. Then you can give the Type as **xlFillSeries** (Excel constant) to fill the series. When this macro executes, we will get a number series from 1 to 10.

You can remove the word destination and write the Range directly like this **Range("A1:A2").AutoFill Range("A1:A10")** if you want.

This is another way of writing the code and it is the better way because of declaring object variables.

Example: Chapter 6.52 - Autofill_Examp2.txt

```
Sub Autofill_Examp2()

Range("A1") = 1

Dim SourceRange As Range
Dim FillRange As Range

Set SourceRange = Worksheets("Sheet1").Range("A1")
Set FillRange = Worksheets("Sheet1").Range("A1:A10")

SourceRange.AutoFill Destination:=FillRange, Type:=xlFillSeries

End Sub
```

Here we have declared the object variables SourceRange and FillRange as Range object. Then we set the cells we are using as source to the variable SourceRange. And FillRange variable is used to set the range to be filled. Then we have used those variables in the place of source and destination in AutoFill method.

Example: Chapter 6.53 - Autofill_Examp3.txt

```
Sub Autofill_Examp3()

Range("A1") = 1
Dim SourceRange1 As Range
Dim FillRange1 As Range
Set SourceRange1 = ActiveSheet.Range("A1")
Set FillRange1 = ActiveSheet.Range("A1:A5")
SourceRange1.AutoFill FillRange1, xlFillSeries

Range("B1") = "Monday"
Dim SourceRange2 As Range
Dim FillRange2 As Range
Set SourceRange2 = ActiveSheet.Range("B1")
Set FillRange2 = ActiveSheet.Range("B1:B5")
```

SourceRange2.AutoFill FillRange2, xlFillWeekdays

Range("C1") = "January"
Dim SourceRange3 As Range
Dim FillRange3 As Range
Set SourceRange3 = ActiveSheet.Range("C1")
Set FillRange3 = ActiveSheet.Range("C1:C5")
SourceRange3.AutoFill FillRange3, xlFillMonths

End Sub

In this example, we have used the type parameter to explicitly tell which series to fill. So this macro will fill the series from 1 to 5 in the cells A1:A5. B1:B5 will be filled with weekdays and C1C5 will be filled with months. You can rewrite the last line of code like this to make it very clear what FillRange and Type are, **SourceRange3.AutoFill Destination:=FillRange3, Type:= xlFillMonths.**

Like this, you can use the type argument as per your requirement.

Here is another example. Before running this macro enter 1 in A1 cell and 2 in B1 cell. This macro is used to fill the data in the current column till the row number based on previous column of the data.

Example: Chapter 6.54 - Autofill Examp4.txt

Sub Autofill_Examp4()

Range("A1").AutoFill Range("A1:A5"), xlFillSeries

Range("B1").Activate

Range("B1").AutoFill Range(ActiveCell, ActiveCell.Offset(0, -1).End(xlDown).Offset(0, 1))

End Sub

Macro will fill the series 1 to 5 in the cell range A1:A5. Then we will activate the B1 cell and fill the value 2 till the end row based on the row number of the left column. For that we have used the Activecell and Offset.

Usually, we can write Range in two ways, **Range("B1:B5")** or **Range(Cells(1, 2), Cells(5, 2))**. But the problem is ending row number is hardcoded. Suppose tomorrow if the A column contains ten rows of data then B column will fill up to fifth row because of hardcoding the row number. So to make it dynamic, we have used the Active cell and Offset.

So instead of writing Range(Cells(1, 2), Cells(5, 2)) we changed the first part to ActiveCell. Since we have selected B1 in the previous line B1 is the active cell. Now instead of second part Cell(5,2) we have used **ActiveCell.Offset(0, -1).End(xlDown).Offset(0, 1)**. Offset(0, -1) will offset one column from the active cell B1 to A1 as we have given the negative column index as -1. Then we have used the End property and the direction xlDown to go to the last cell down. Now again we offset from the last cell to next column by specifying Offset(0, 1). Because we have given 1 as column number, it will go to the next column B.

So this **Range(ActiveCell, ActiveCell.Offset(0, -1).End(xlDown).Offset(0, 1))** will inturn give the range Range(Cells(1, 2), Cells(5, 2)).

So here we have one line of code that we can use to Auto Fill down from any active cell without specifying the row number.

You can fill upwards also to the first row from the last cell or the cell you specify. For that, you can change the code like this, **Range("B6").AutoFill Range(ActiveCell, ActiveCell.Offset(0, -1).End(xlUp).Offset(0, 1))**. First, activate B6 cell using Range("B6").Activate and write the above code. This will fill the data upwards.

Below example allows the user to give the destination cell range. For that, we are using InputBox.

Example: Chapter 6.55 - Autofill_Examp5.txt

Sub Autofill_Examp5()

Dim YourRange As String

Range("A1").CurrentRegion.ClearContents

YourRange = InputBox("Enter your range")
Range("A1") = 1
Range("A1").AutoFill Destination:=Range(YourRange), Type:=xlFillSeries

End Sub

First we have declared a string variable **YourRange** to hold the cell range. Then we used ClearContents method to clear the contents of the existing cell range. For that we have used **Range("A1").CurrentRegion.ClearContents. CurrentRegion** from A1 will select the entire data starting from A1 cell and ClearContents will clear the data.

Enter the value A1:A10 or A1:A100 in the Input box and you will get the series filled in the range.

AutoFilter Method

AutoFilter method is used for filtering the data, same as Excel's Filter under Data tab.

Syntax:

expression .AutoFilter(Field, Criteria1, Operator, Criteria2, VisibleDropDown)

Parameters:

All these parameters are optional

Field - the column you want to filter. You can specify an Integer. If Range starts from A column, then A column is 1 B column is 2.

Criteria1 - the criteria you want to filter with, For example, if you want to filter with 10. Use "=" to find blank fields, or use "<>" to find nonblank fields.

Operator - It specifies the type of filter. Some of the operators commonly used are listed below.

xlAnd, value is 1 and is the logical AND of Criteria1 and Criteria2.

xlBottom10Items, value is 4 and lowest-valued items displayed (number of items specified in Criteria1).

xlBottom10Percent, value is 6 and Lowest-valued items displayed (percentage specified in Criteria1).

xlFilterCellColor, value is 8 and Color of the cell

xlFilterDynamic, value is 11 and Dynamic filter

xlFilterFontColor, value is 9 and Color of the font

xlFilterIcon, value is 10 and Filter icon

xlFilterValues, value is 7 and Filter values

xlOr value is 2 and Logical OR of Criteria1 or Criteria2.

xlTop10Items is 3 and Highest-valued items displayed (number of items specified in Criteria1).

xlTop10Percent is 5 Highest-valued items displayed (percentage specified in Criteria1).

Criteria2 - The second criteria used with Criteria1 and Operator to construct compound criteria.

VisibleDropDown - False to hide the Filter drop-down arrow for the filtered field. True by default.

Example: Chapter 6.56 - AutoFilterExamp1.txt

Here we have students list like this in the image. You can open the Excel file Chapter 6.56 - AutoFilterExamp1.xlsx to work along.

	A	B	C	D	E
1	Roll no.	Name	Age	Subject	Score
2	2	Sam	21	Physics	65
3	6	Mily	21	Physics	85
4	9	John	21	Physics	95
5	10	Lucy	21	Physics	75
6	2	Sam	21	Chemistry	45
7	6	Mily	21	Chemistry	38
8	9	John	21	Chemistry	78
9	10	Lucy	21	Chemistry	99

Sub AutoFilterExamp1()

Range("A1:E1").AutoFilter Field:=4, Criteria1:="Physics"

End Sub

If you run this macro, you will get the data filtered with the subject Physics. First, we have given the range to filter in the auto filter method like this **Range("A1:E1").AutoFilter**. Then we gave the column you want to filter, for that you can give the column number in the Field parameter. Since Subject is the fourth column, you can give 4. Then you can give the text you want to filter with. Here you want to filter with Physics so you give Physics as Criteria1.

Now if you want to filter by students marks above 70. Then you can change the code like this **Range("A1:E1").AutoFilter Field:=5, Criteria1:=">70"**. Before running this code make sure the data is not in filtered mode. Either you remove the filter manually or add this line of code **ActiveSheet.AutoFilterMode = False** to remove the filter. So final code will look like this.

Example: Chapter 6.57 - AutoFilterExamp2.txt

Sub AutoFilterExamp2()

ActiveSheet.AutoFilterMode = False

Range("A1:E1").AutoFilter Field:=5, Criteria1:=">70"

End Sub

Now if you want to filter the names starting with letter "M" from the name, then you can change the Field and Criteria like this.

Field:=2, Criteria1:="=M*"

Star sign will search for whatever name starting with M and rest of the letters can be anything. Be it Mily or Melvin or Michael.

Using two Criteria

Example: Chapter 6.58 - AutoFilterExamp3.txt

Sub AutoFilterExamp3()

ActiveSheet.AutoFilterMode = False

Range("A1:E1").AutoFilter Field:=5, Criteria1:=">=60", Operator:=xlAnd, Criteria2:="<=90"

End Sub

This example we have filtered the score between 60 and 90. For that, we have used the third parameter Operator and gave the constant xlAnd. So if these two criteria are correct, that score is filtered.

Using Autofilter on two different Columns

Example: Chapter 6.59 - AutoFilterExamp4.txt

```
Sub AutoFilterExamp4()

ActiveSheet.AutoFilterMode = False

Range("A1:E1").AutoFilter Field:=4, Criteria1:="Physics"

Range("A1:E1").AutoFilter Field:=5, Criteria1:=">=60"

End Sub
```

Here we have first filtered with the subject and then with the score above 60. You can add more columns of fields for filtering. But you should not exceed the column count you have given in the Range. Here the column count is 5 from A to E.

You can rewrite the above example using With construct. In this case, you have to specify the range only once. Also, I have added the last parameter VisibleDropDown:=False, so there will not be any drop down menu for the filter for Subject and Score.

Example: Chapter 6.60 - AutoFilterExamp5.txt

```
Sub AutoFilterExamp5()

ActiveSheet.AutoFilterMode = False

With Range("A1:E1")

.AutoFilter Field:=4, Criteria1:="Physics", VisibleDropDown:=False
.AutoFilter Field:=5, Criteria1:=">=60", VisibleDropDown:=False

End With

End Sub
```


Copying filtered data to Sheet2

Example: Chapter 6.61 - AutoFilterExamp6.txt

```
Sub AutoFilterExamp6()

Dim rng As Range

ActiveSheet.AutoFilterMode = False

With Range("A1:E1")
```

```
.AutoFilter Field:=4, Criteria1:="Physics", VisibleDropDown:=False
.AutoFilter Field:=5, Criteria1:=">=60", VisibleDropDown:=False

End With

Worksheets("Sheet2").Cells.Clear

Set rng = ActiveSheet.AutoFilter.Range

rng.Offset(1, 0).Copy _

Destination:=Worksheets("Sheet2").Range("A1")

End Sub
```

Here we are copying the filtered data using the Copy method. The first section filters the data. Then we have declared a range object variable rng and assigned with **ActiveSheet.AutoFilter.Range**, so it will always refer to the filtered range. We have used Offset property and mentioned the row offset as 1. This will ensure the heading is skipped and the data after the heading is copied. If you want the heading also, set the Offset property to **Offset(0, 0).**

Points to note:

We have used a space and an underscore to split multiple lines of codes to single line where copy method is used.

ClearHyperlinks

Using ClearHyperlinks method is equivalent to using the Clear Hyperlinks command from the **Clear drop-down list** in the Editing section of the Home tab. Only hyperlinks will be removed; all other cell content, such as text and formatting will be unaffected.

Example: Chapter 6.62 - ClearHyperExamp.txt

```
Sub ClearHyperExamp()

Range("A1").CurrentRegion.ClearHyperlinks

End Sub
```

This example will clear all the hyperlinks from the current region of A1 cell (CurrentRegion property will select all the cells having the data till there is blank row or column). Now if you want you can specify a range like this **Range("A1:A10").ClearHyperlinks**, it will clear all the Hyperlinks in the range A1:A10.

FillDown

This method fills down from the top cell or cells in the specified range to the bottom of the range. The contents and formatting of the cell or cells in the top row of a range are copied into the rest of the rows in the range.

Example: Chapter 6.63 - FillDownExamp.txt

Sub FillDownExamp()

Range("B1:B10").FillDown

End Sub

Enter the value 25 in B1 cell and run this macro. It will fill the value from B1:B10.

FillLeft

This method fills left from the rightmost cell or cells in the specified range. The contents and formatting of the cell or cells in the rightmost column of a range are copied into the rest of the columns in the range.

Example: Chapter 6.64 - FillLeftExamp.txt

Sub FillLeftExamp()

Range("B10:H10").FillLeft

End Sub

Enter the value 75 in the cell H10 and run this macro. This macro fills the range B10:H10 with the contents of the cell H10.

FillRight

This method fills right from the leftmost cell or cells in the specified range. The contents and formatting of the cell or cells in the leftmost column of a range are copied into the rest of the columns in the range.

Example: Chapter 6.65 - FillRightExamp.txt

Sub FillRightExamp()

Range("B10:H10").FillRight

End Sub

Enter the value 75 in the cell B10 and change the font color to red and run this macro. This macro fills the range B10:H10 with the contents of the cell B10.

FillUp

This method fills up from the bottom cell or cells in the specified range. The contents and formatting of the cell or cells in the bottom cell of a range are copied into the rest of the rows in the range.

Example: Chapter 6.66 - FillUpExamp.txt

Sub FillUpExamp()

Range("B2:B25").FillUp

End Sub

Enter the value 75 in the cell B25 and change the font color to red and run this macro. This macro fills the range B2:B25 with the contents of the cell B25.

Merge

Merge method is used to merge multiple cells into single one. Keep in mind the merging will result in loss of data.

Syntax:

Range("MyRange").Merge ([Across])

The default value of across is False and true will merge cells in each row of the specified range as separate merged cells.

Example: Chapter 6.67 - MergeCells1.txt

Sub MergeCells1()

Range("A1:C5").Merge

End Sub

Here we have not mentioned the across value so it will be false. This will merge the whole cells into a single cell A1. See the image below after merging.

Example: Chapter 6.68 - MergeCells1.txt

Sub MergeCells1()

Range("A1:C5").Merge True

End Sub

By specifying the across value as True, it will merge each row separately. See the image below after merging.

PasteSpecial Method

This method can be used to paste values, formulas, formats, etc.

Syntax:

Range.PasteSpecial(Paste, Operation, SkipBlanks, Transpose)

Parameters:

All these parameters are optional

Paste - You can specify the type you want to paste. You can use **xlPasteFormats** for copying source format. Or use **xlPasteFormulas** for pasting formulas. Or use **xlPasteValues** for pasting values only. You can get the complete list from the Excel's help menu by clicking F1.

Operation - XlPasteSpecialOperation . Determines whether the copied data will be added or subtracted or divided or multiplied.

SkipBlanks - Determines blank cells in the range on the Clipboard not be pasted into the destination range. The default value is False.

Transpose - transpose rows and columns when the range is pasted. The default value is False.

Example: Chapter 6.69 - PasteSpecialExamp1.txt

Open the file Chapter 6.69 - PasteSpecialExamp1.xlsx to work along.

Sub PasteSpecialExamp1()

Range("A1").Copy
Range("B1").PasteSpecial Paste:=xlPasteFormats

Range("A2").Copy
Range("B2").PasteSpecial Paste:=xlPasteValues

Worksheets("Sheet1").Range("A3").Copy
Worksheets("Sheet1").Range("B3").PasteSpecial Paste:=xlPasteFormulas

End Sub

We have the values 25 in A1, 45 in A2 and the sum of A1 and A2, 70 in A3 cell. Now if you run this macro A1 cell will be copied and is pasted to B1 cell. I have specified the constant **xlPasteFormats** as the argument, so only formats will be copied. Here the background color is yellow so that color will be copied.

Like that **xlPasteValues** will paste values only and **xlPasteFormulas** will paste only formulas. Run the macro and see yourself what you get.

Now if you want to paste value into sheet2, you can change the last line of code like this **Worksheets("Sheet2").Range("B3").PasteSpecial Paste:= xlPasteValues.**

Paste Special using Transpose

Example: Chapter 6.70 - PasteSpecialExamp2.txt

Sub PasteSpecialExamp2()

Range("A1:A6").Copy

Range("B1").PasteSpecial Paste:=xlValues, Transpose:=True

End Sub

Before running the macro fill the cells A1:A6 with some values and then run this macro. Data will be transposed to horizontal position starting from cell B1.

Paste Special using Skipblanks

Here we have data like this in the image. Now open file Chapter 6.71 PasteSpecialExamp3.xlsx and run this macro given.

Image before running macro.

	A	B
1	1	
2	2	100
3	3	
4	4	
5	5	500
6	6	

Example: Chapter 6.71 PasteSpecialExamp3.txt

Sub PasteSpecialExamp3()

Range("B1:B6").Copy
Range("A1").PasteSpecial Paste:=xlValues, skipblanks:=True
Application.CutCopyMode = False

End Sub

Image after running macro

	A	B
1	1	
2	100	100
3	3	
4	4	
5	500	500
6	6	

Here cells from B1:B6 are copied to A1 cell. Because we have mentioned the skipblanks as true, it will not paste the blank cells to the Range A1:A6. Last we have mentioned **Application.CutCopyMode = False** to remove the marching ants from the range B1:B6.

More about referencing to Cells

Here we are going through some more examples of the Cells property. Earlier we have gone through the cell property of the Range object. But here we are referring to the Applications cells property. The application also has a cells property. So don't confuse with the Range objects cells property.

Example: Chapter 6.72 - UsingCells.txt

```
Sub UsingCells()

Cells(1, 1) = 100

End Sub
```

Here we are using the Cells property to assign the value 100 to A1 cell. The first **1** after the bracket is the row number and the second **1** is the column number. So if you want to enter the value 100 in B1, you have to change the code to Cells(1, 2).

Here we have skipped the Object name Application and used only the Property name. You can write the object name also if you want **Application.Cells(1, 1) = 100**. In Excel, column number comes first followed by the row number like this A1. Here in Cells property, it is the row which comes first.

The power of cells property is you can you can dynamically input the values using a Loop.

Let's look into an example. Here we have used loop and entered the value 100 in the range A1:A10.

Example: Chapter 6.73 - UsingCells1.txt

```
Sub UsingCells1()

Dim i As Integer

For i = 1 To 10
Cells(i, 1) = 100
Next

End Sub
```


Example: Chapter 6.74 - CellsCheck.txt

```
Sub CellsCheck()

Dim i As Integer

Dim InputValue As Integer

InputValue = 100

For i = 1 To 10

Application.Cells(i, 1) = InputValue

InputValue = InputValue + 1

Next i

End Sub
```

99

Like the example written before, you don't want to write the word Application. You can just write **Cells(i, 1) = InputValue** and get away with it because here Excel is our Application. Why I have specified this once more is to remove the confusion from your mind as we are using the cells property of Application object, not Range object. If you want to use the range object you have to write **Range(Cells(i, 1), Cells(i, 1)).Value = InputValue.**

More examples are given below for you to understand the cells property. This one will add the value in the cell B3 to cell C5 and then Message box will display the content on cell C5. Enter a value in cell B3 and run this macro.

Example: Chapter 6.75 - CellsAdd.txt

Sub CellsAdd()

Cells(5, 3) = Cells(3, 2)

MsgBox Cells(5, 3)

End Sub

This one will add the value from the cell B3 to the cell C5 and then display the value of the cell C5. Enter a value in cell B3 and run this macro.

Example: Chapter 6.76 - CellReadWrite.txt

Sub CellReadWrite()

Cells(5,3) = Sheets("Sheet1").Range("B3")

MsgBox Cells(5,3)

End Sub

You can rewrite the macro like this also.

Example: Chapter 6.77 – CellReadWrite1.txt

Sub CellReadWrite1 ()

Sheets("Sheet1").Cells(5,3) = Range("B3")

MsgBox Sheets("Sheet1").Cells(5,3)

End Sub

So by using cells property, you can reach any cell in the Excel dynamically. We will look into another practical example which you encounter every day.

We have a data like in this image given below. Here, we want to insert the percentage in F column. Open the Excel file Chapter 6.78 – PercentageCalc.xlsx to work along.

Example: Chapter 6.78 – PercentageCalc.txt

	A	B	C	D	E
1	Division	Student Name	Subject	Month	Score
2	A	John	Physics	Jan	25
3	B	Hary	Physics	Feb	35
4	A	Lucy	Physics	Mar	85
5	B	Bell	Physics	April	72
6	A	Ancy	Maths	Jan	92
7	B	Liza	Maths	Feb	66
8	A	Tom	Maths	Mar	54
9	B	Melvin	Maths	April	49

For that, you can write a Sub procedure like this.

Sub PercentageCalc ()

Range("F1").Value = "Percentage"
Range("F2:F9").Value = "=E2*100%"

End Sub

Now if you are getting the data with same row numbers every day, this Macro will work. In other words, we have hardcoded the row number. But if the number of rows varies, then this macro will not work. So for that, you have to make changes to get the percentage dynamically like this.

Example: Chapter 6.79 – PercentageCalc1.txt

Sub PercentageCalc1()

Dim LastRow As Long
Dim LastColumn As Long
Dim i As Long

LastRow = ActiveSheet.UsedRange.Rows.count
LastColumn = ActiveSheet.UsedRange.Columns.count

LastColumn = LastColumn + 1

For i = 2 To LastRow
Cells(i, LastColumn).Value = Cells(i, LastColumn - 1) * 100 / 100
Next

Cells(1, LastColumn).Value = "Percentage"

End Sub

Here we have declared three variables **LastRow**, **LastColumn** and **i**. LastRow is used for storing the number of rows, LastColumn for number of Columns and i for looping purpose. Then we found out the used row and column using UsedRange property of the Worksheet object and stored in LastRow and LastColumn variable. Then we add up the LastColumn variable to get the non used column which is F column. Then we use a loop to populate the percentage and given the name **Percentage** to F1 cell. This macro will work even if the column number increases.

Chapter 7

Built-In VBA Functions

To get a list of VBA functions while you're writing your code, type VBA followed by a period (.). The VBE displays list of all its members, including functions preceded by a green icon.

If this doesn't work check the Auto List Members option is selected. Choose Tools Image from book Options and then click the Editor tab.

Message Functions

MsgBox

The MsgBox is a dialog box will give a pop up with the message you assigned to display.

Example: Chapter 7.1 - MsgboxExamp1.txt

Sub MsgboxExamp1()

MsgBox "Hello World"

End Sub

You will get a message box with the text Hello World if you execute this macro.

Given below is another example, before executing this, you have to insert 25 in the cell A1.

Example: Chapter 7.2 – MsgboxExamp2.txt

Sub MsgboxExamp2()

MsgBox "Range A1 value is " & Range("A1").Value

End Sub

You will get the value stored in A1 cell.

Example: Chapter 7.3 – MsgboxExamp3.txt

Sub MsgboxExamp3()

MsgBox "First Line" & vbNewLine & "Second Line"

End Sub

This one we will get the answer like this in the image given below. We use the vbNewLine constant to start a new line. The two string are concatenated using the & operator with vbNewLine constant in between.

Now we will go through the syntax of the MsgBox.

Syntax:

MsgBox(prompt[, buttons] [, title] [, helpfile, context])

Parameters:

First parameter is required, rest all are optional.

prompt - this is the text message displayed in the dialog box. The Maximum length of Prompt is 1024 Characters. You can use carriage return Character If prompt consists more than one line.

buttons - It Contains Numeric value specifying the number and type of buttons to display. The default button value is 0.

title- This is the title or name of the dialog box.

helpfile - String expression that identifies the Help file to use to offer context-sensitive Help for the dialog box. If helpfile is provided, context must also be provided.

context - Numeric expression that is the Help context number assigned to the appropriate Help topic by the Help author. If context is provided, helpfile must also be provided.

Example: Chapter 7.4 – MsgboxExamp4.txt

Sub MsgboxExamp4()

MsgBox "Hello World", vbOKCancel, "My Title"

End Sub

If you don't specify any value in the button, you will get an OK button. But if you specify as in the above example as vbOKCancel, then you will get Ok and Cancel. Instead of VbOKCancel you can use the numeric value of the constants. Numeric values of some constants are given below with the purpose.

vbOKOnly - numeric value is 0 and displays OK button only.

vbOKCancel - numeric value is 1 and displays OK and Cancel buttons.

vbAbortRetryIgnore - numeric value is 2 and displays Abort, Retry, and Ignore buttons.

vbYesNoCancel - numeric value is 3 and displays Yes, No, and Cancel buttons.

vbYesNo - numeric value is 4 and displays Yes and No buttons.

There are also other values for the button which you can find out from Excels help menu.

These are the return values of the button when you click Ok or Cancel or Abort

vbOK value is 1 for OK

vbCancel value is 2 for Cancel

vbAbort value is 3 for Abort

vbRetry value is 4 for Retry

vbIgnore value is 5 for Ignore

vbYes value is 6 for Yes

vbNo value is 7 for No

Example: Chapter 7.5 – MsgboxExamp5.txt

```
Sub MsgboxExamp5()

If MsgBox("Hello World", vbOKCancel, "My Title") = vbCancel Then
MsgBox "You have clicked Cancel button."
End If

End Sub
```

In this example, when you run the above macro, you will get two buttons Ok and Cancel because of using the vbOKCancel. Now if you click the cancel, IF condition will check Cancel button is clicked and will process the statement inside IF, which is another Msgbox function. For checking Cancel button is clicked we have used another constant vbCancel.

Example: Chapter 7.6 – MsgboxExamp6.txt

```
Sub MsgboxExamp6()

Dim message As String

message = MsgBox("Hi, Are you a bachelor? Click" _
& vbCr & "Yes: I'am a bachelor." _
& vbCr & "No: I'am not a bachelor." _
& vbCr & "Cancel: Not Interested" _
, vbYesNoCancel + vbQuestion)

If message = vbYes Then
MsgBox "You are welcome"

ElseIf message = vbNo Then
MsgBox "You are not welcome"

ElseIf message = vbCancel Then
MsgBox "Thank you"

End If

End Sub
```

Here we have declared a variable called message as string to hold the question we are asking. We have used vbCr to split the question to separate lines. vbCr is a constant in VBA for carriage return. Then we used the button vbYesNoCancel to get the button with Yes, No and Cancel. We have used the + sign to add vbQuestion to display Warning Query icon. Run the macro and see what you are getting.

InputBox

Use InputBox to display a simple dialog box to enter information to be used in a macro. The dialog box has an OK button and a Cancel button. If you choose the OK button, InputBox returns the value entered in the dialog box. If you click the Cancel button, InputBox returns False.

There are two Inputbox methods. First one is Excel VBA's Inputbox and the second one is Applications, means Excel itself. We will look into the first one here.

VBA's Inputbox

This function displays an Inputbox requesting the user the enter a value.

Syntax:

InputBox(prompt[, title] [, default] [, xpos] [, ypos] [, helpfile, context])

Each parameter is explained below first parameter is Mandatory and rest of the parameters are optional.

prompt - this is the message you want to display in the InputBox. The Maximum length of Prompt is 1024 Characters. You can use carriage return Character If prompt consists more than one line.

title - this is the title or name of the Inputbox.

default - default value which you can give. If there is no default value Inputbox will be empty.

xpos - numeric expression that specifies the horizontal distance of the left edge of the dialog box from the left edge of the screen. If xpos is omitted, the dialog box is horizontally centered.

ypos - numeric expression that specifies the vertical distance of the upper edge of the dialog box from the top of the screen. If ypos is omitted, the dialog box is vertically positioned approximately one-third of the way down the screen.

helpfile - string expression that identifies the Help file to use to provide context-sensitive Help for the dialog box. If helpfile is provided, context must also be provided.

context - numeric expression that is the Help context number assigned to the appropriate Help topic by the Help author. If the context is provided, helpfile must also be provided.

Example: Chapter 7.7 – InputExamp.txt

Sub InputExamp ()

Dim InputValue As Variant

InputValue = InputBox("Please enter your name")

InputValue = InputBox("Please enter your name", "Name")

InputValue = InputBox("Please enter your name", "Name", "Sam")

InputValue = InputBox("Please enter your name", Title:="Name", Default:="Sam")

InputValue = InputBox("Please enter your name", Title:="Name", Default:="Sam", Xpos:=15, Ypos:=45)

End Sub

Here we have declared the variable InputValue as Variant to hold the values we get from Inputbox. When you run this program you will get five types of Input box.

First one will be with the prompt, 'Please enter your name'. Second one with Prompt and Title, Name. Third one with Prompt, Title and Default value Sam. Fourth one I have rewritten the third one with named parameters to make it clear what is Name and Sam.

Named parameters means you can give the name of the parameter followed by colon and equal sign. And then you can specify the value so it will be clear what you are specifying.

The fifth one I have included the X and Y position at which you want to show the Input box. Click OK or Cancel one after the other to get the five Inputboxes.

Application's Inputbox

The biggest difference is that the Application specific input box has an extra Type argument which is very useful. This InputBox function allows selective validation of the user's input.

Syntax:

InputBox(prompt, title, default, left, top, helpFile, helpContextID, type)

Parameters:

First parameter is mandatory and rest are optional.

prompt - this is the message you want to display.

title - this is the title for the input box and if omitted, the default title is "Input."

default - default value displayed inside the Inpubox.

left - specifies an x position for the dialog box in relation to the upper-left corner of the screen

top - specifies a y position for the dialog box in relation to the upper-left corner of the screen, in points.

helpFile - the name of the Help file for this input box. If the HelpFile and HelpContextID arguments are present, a Help button will appear in the dialog box.

helpContextID - the context ID number of the Help topic in HelpFile.

type - the return data type. If this argument is omitted, the dialog box returns text.

These are the values that can be passed in the Type argument. Can be one or a sum of the values. For example, for an input box that can accept both text and numbers, set Type to 1 + 2.

0 is formula.

1 is number.

2 is Text (a string).

4 is logical value (True or False).

8 is cell reference, as a Range object.

16 is an error value, such as #N/A.

64 is an array of values.

Checking the value is numeric using Application's InputBox

Example: Chapter 7.8 – InputExamp1.txt

Sub InputExamp1()

Dim varInput As Variant

varInput = Application.InputBox(Prompt:="Enter a number:", Type:=1)

If varInput <> False Then

End If

End Sub

Here we have declared a variant variable **varInput** to store the value from InputBox. In the Input box, we have given the Type Parameter as 1. This will check whether the entered variable is number or not. If it is not number you will be prompted with an error message **Number is not valid.**

After clicking OK on the Number is not valid message, the user will get a chance to enter the number again. This type of error checking is not there in the VBA's Inputbox. In other words, you don't have to write codes for checking whether the user entered a number or not in Application's Inputbox.

Checking the value is Range using Application.InputBox

By specifying the Type as 8, the input box will automatically check whether the input is a range. If it is not a range, it will again prompt you for a number. Here if you click cancel it will go the error label DisplayError and give you the error message **You didn't choose anything!".**

Example: Chapter 7.9 – InputExamp2.txt

```
Sub InputExamp2()

Dim MyRange As Range

On Error GoTo DisplayError

Set MyRange = Application.InputBox(prompt:="Select a range ", Type:=8)

MyRange.Select

Exit Sub

DisplayError:

MsgBox "You didn't choose anything!"

End Sub
```

Other functions

Shell

Shell commands can run executable commands (exe). You don't need to reference the path to the exe as long as you know the name. Here are few examples. Select Shell and press F1 to get detailed help on Shell from VBE.

Example: Chapter 7.10 - ShellExamp1.txt

```
Sub ShellExamp1()

Dim retVal As String

retVal = Shell("Notepad.exe", vbNormalFocus)

End Sub
```

Example: Chapter 7.11 - ShellExamp1.txt

```
Sub ShellExamp2()

Dim retVal As String

retVal = Shell("calc.exe", vbMaximizedFocus)

End Sub
```

Example: Chapter 7.12 - ShellExamp1.txt

```
Sub ShellExamp3()
Dim retVal As String
retVal = Shell("WinWord.exe", vbNormalFocus)
End Sub
```

VBA Text Functions

Format

This function applies a format to an expression and returns the result as a string.

Syntax:

Format(expression[,format])

Parameters:

expression - the numeric value to format.

format - Optional parameter. It is the format to apply. You can either define your own format or use one of the named formats in Excel. Given below are the formats.

General Number - Displays a number without thousand separators.

Currency - Displays thousand separators as well as two decimal places.

Fixed - Displays at least one digit to the left of the decimal place and two digits to the right of the decimal place.

Standard - Displays the thousand separators, at least one digit to the left of the decimal place, and two digits to the right of the decimal place.

Percent - Displays a percent value, a number multiplied by 100 with a percent sign. Displays two digits to the right of the decimal place.

Scientific - Scientific notation.

Yes/No - Displays No if the number is 0. Displays Yes if the number is not 0.

True/False - Displays False if the number is 0. Displays True if the number is not 0.

On/Off - Displays Off if the number is 0. Displays On if the number is not 0.

Example: Chapter 7.13 - FormatExamp.txt

Sub FormatExamp()

```
Dim FormatValue As Integer
Dim Result As String
FormatValue = 351.8

Result = Format(FormatValue, "General Number")
MsgBox "General Number " & Result

Result = Format(FormatValue, "Currency")
MsgBox "Currency Format " & Result

Result = Format(FormatValue, "Fixed")
MsgBox "Fixed Format " & Result

Result = Format(FormatValue, "Standard")
MsgBox "Standard Format " & Result

Result = Format(FormatValue, "Percent")
MsgBox "Percent Format " & Result

Result = Format(FormatValue, "#,##0.00")
MsgBox "Custom Format " & Result

End Sub
```

Here we have declared two variables FormatValue as Integer and Result as String. Then we stored the number 351.8 in the FormatValue. Then the same is formatted using Format function and stored in Result variable and displayed using Msgbox. Last one we have put a custom format.

Len

This function returns the length of a string. For example, if the text is Sam, it will return three and if it is James, it will return four.

Syntax:

LEN(text)

Example: Chapter 7.14 - Len_Examp.txt

```
Sub Len_Examp()

Dim Name As String
Name = "James Cameron"

MsgBox ("Total length of the Name is " & Len(Name))

End Sub
```

InStr

This will returns the position of a character or characters within a text as integer. In other words, it will search a word or an alphabet inside a word or sentence and then returns the starting position number.

Syntax:

InStr([Start], String1, String2, [Compare])

Parameters:

[Start] - optional integer argument, representing the position that you want to start searching from. If omitted, the [Start] argument takes on the default value of 1.

String1 - the string that you want to search.

String2 - the substring that you want to search for.

[Compare] - Optional argument, specifying the type of comparison to make, can be any of the following values:

vbBinaryCompare - performs a binary comparison.
vbTextCompare - performs a text comparison.

vbDatabaseCompare - performs a database comparison.

If omitted, the [Compare] argument takes on the default value vbBinaryCompare.

Example: Chapter 7.15 - InStr_Examp.txt

Sub InStr_Examp()

Dim Result As Integer

Result = InStr("Welcome to merina", "me")
MsgBox Result

Result = InStr(7, "Welcome to merina", "me")
MsgBox Result

Result = InStr(1, "Welcome to merina", "w")
MsgBox Result

End Sub

You will get the answer 6 from the first Msgbox, the word 'me' starts at 6 in the sentence "Welcome to merina".

In the second one, I have put the start position (first parameter) as 7. Now you will get the answer 12. It will skip the first 'me' as it starts in the 6th letter whereas we have given the 7th letter as the starting position.

Third, we are searching the letter 'w'; Since InStr is case sensitive, you will get the answer 0.

InStrRev

This function will return an integer representing the position of a substring within a string, searching from right to left (i.e., from the end to the start of the string). If the substring is not found, the function returns the value 0. This function is the same as InStr, but the difference is that InStrRev starts the search from the end of the string rather than the beginning.

Syntax:

InStrRev(StringCheck, StringMatch, [Start], [Compare])

Parameters:

StringCheck - the string that you want to search.

StringMatch - the substring that you want to search for.

[Start] - optional integer argument, representing the position (from the start of StringCheck) that you want to start searching from. If omitted, the [Start] argument takes on the default value of -1, meaning that the search starts from the end of the string.

[Compare] - An optional argument representing the type of comparison to make. If omitted, the [Compare] argument takes on the default value vbBinaryCompare.

Compare can be any of the following values.

vbBinaryCompare - performs a binary comparison
vbTextCompare - performs a text comparison
vbDatabaseCompare - performs a database comparison

Example: Chapter 7.16 - InStrRev_Examp.txt

Sub InStrRev_Examp()

Dim Result As Integer

Result = InStrRev("Welcome to merina", "me")
MsgBox Result

Result = InStrRev("Welcome to merina", "me", 7)
MsgBox Result

Result = InStrRev("Welcome to merina", "w")
MsgBox Result

End Sub

First message box you will get the answer 12. Here the search starts from the right and first **me** from right is in the word merina and it is 12th character from the right.

Second message box you will get the answer 6. The search starts from the seventh character from the right and **me** is in the word Welcome. And m starts from the sixth position.

Third, we are searching the letter 'w'; Since InStrRev is case sensitive, you will get the answer 0.

Left, Right

The left function is used to get a specified number of characters of a text from the left side whereas Right function is used to get the specified number of characters of a text from the right side. These functions are similar to the worksheet functions Left and Right.

Syntax:

1.   Left(string, length)

2.   Right(string. Length)

Parameters:

Both have these common parameters

string – the text you want to search.

length - how many characters you want to get.

In this example, we want to separate the email id and the email provider, i.e., Ymail or Gmail or Hotmail.

Example: Chapter 7.17 - Left_Right1.txt

Sub Left_Right1 ()

Dim Email As String

Email = "exceltovba@ymail.com"

MsgBox Left(Email, 10)
MsgBox Right(Email, 9)

End Sub

If you run this macro, you will get two message boxes with **exceltovba** and **ymail.**

The left function will extract the first ten characters from the string exceltovba and Right function will extract nine characters from the right side of the string.

Now the above example is not dynamic because Email address will be of different length. So we can rewrite this macro like this.

Example: Chapter 7.18 - Left_Right2.txt

Sub Left_Right2()

Dim Email As String
Dim Seperator As Integer

Email = "exceltovba@ymail.com"

Seperator = InStr(Email, "@")

MsgBox ("Email id is: " & Left(Email, Seperator - 1))

MsgBox ("Email Provider is: " & Right(Email, Len(Email) - Seperator))

End Sub

Here we have declared two variables Email as String and Seperator as Integer. Email for holding the text **exceltovba@ymail.com** and Seperator for holding the number of characters at which the @ symbol starts.

Then we used the InStr function to get the starting position of the '@' symbol which is 11.

In the first Message box, we used the Left function and the splitting number we gave as Seperator – 1 which will workout to 10. So Left function will get the first ten characters which is the first portion of the email id.

In the second Message box, we used the Right function. We don't know the starting position of @ symbol from right. So indirectly we find out where the @ symbol starts. We use the Len function to get the full length of the text and then deduct the Separator value from it. The total length of the text exceltovba@ymail.com is 20 and when you deduct the separator value 11, you will get 9. This is supplied as second parameter of the right function.

Now the beauty of the above macro is you can write a For loop and separate the email id and provider from a range. In the above example, we have assigned the email directly like this, **Email = exceltovba@ymail.com.** Instead, you can directly get it from a cell by writing Email = Range("A1").value. Try it for yourself.

LCase , UCase

LCase converts a supplied string to lower case text and UCase converts a supplied string to upper case text.

Syntax:

LCase(text)

UCase(text)

Text – the text you want to convert.

Example: Chapter 7.19 - ChangeCaseExamp.txt

First, enter the text **This is fun** in capital letters in A1 cell and small letters in A2 cell.

Sub ChangeCaseExamp()

Range("B1").Value = LCase(Range("A1").Value)

Range("B2").Value = UCase(Range("A2").Value)

End Sub

Write this code in VBE and run. You will get lowercase text in cell B1 and uppercase text in B2.

LTrim, RTrim

LTrim removes leading spaces from a supplied string and RTrim removes trailing spaces from a supplied string.

Syntax:

LTrim(text)

RTrim (text)

text- text you want to trim

Example: Chapter 7.20 - LRtrim_Examp.txt

Sub LRtrim_Examp()

Dim Text1 As String
Dim Text2 As String
Dim Result As String

Text1 = "   Hello world."
Text2 = "Hello World.   "

```
MsgBox "Text1 " & Text1
MsgBox "Text2 " & Text2

Result = LTrim(Text1)
MsgBox Result
Result = RTrim(Text2)
MsgBox Result

End Sub
```

We have created three variables Tex1 and Text 2 for holding the word Hello World, Result variable for holding the text after trimming. When you run this macro Ltrim will trim the leading space and you will get the answer **Hello world.** Rtrim will trim the trailing space and still you will get the answer **Hello world.** Please make a note that these two function will not trim any spaces in the middle of the text. For example, if you are trimming the text **Hello world,** you will have the same space after trimming. You can club with Range object to get the text from cell ranges and use this function.

Trim

If you want to trim the leading and trailing spaces from a supplied string, use this function.

Syntax:

Trim(text)

text- text you want to trim

Example: Chapter 7.21 - Trim_Examp.txt

```
Sub Trim_Examp()

Dim Name As String
Name = "    James Alexander   "

MsgBox ("This is before trimming " & Name)
MsgBox ("This is after trimming " & Trim(Name))

Name = "James    Alexander"

MsgBox ("This is before trimming " & Name)
MsgBox ("This is after trimming " & Trim(Name))

End Sub
```

First, we have declared the String **Name** to hold the value **James Alexander**. As you can see, there is space at the beginning and end. Once we trim the text that space will be gone.

Again we have reassigned the **Name** with James Alexander with four space in between, first and second name without any leading and trailing space. But trim will not trim the spaces in the middle of the text.

Mid

This function returns a substring from the middle of a supplied string.

Syntax:

Mid(Str, Start, [Length])

Parameters:

Str – the text you want to extract the characters from.

Start – start position of the character or characters.

[Length] – optional argument, the length of the characters you want. If this is omitted returns all characters from the Start position to the end of the string.

Example: Chapter 7.22 - Mid_Examp.txt

Sub Mid_Examp()

Dim Name As String

Name = "James Alexander"

MsgBox Mid(Name, 7, 4)

End Sub

This example will extract characters from the starting position 7 mentioned as second argument up to 4 characters to right. You will get the answer **Alex**.

Replace

This function replaces a substring within a supplied text string.

Syntax:

Replace(expression, find, replace[, start[, count[, compare]]])

Parameters

Expression – text containing the characters to replace.

Find – characters we are searching for.

Replace – replacing characters which we find using second argument.

Start – optional -Position where search is to begin. If omitted, 1 is assumed.

Count - optional. Number of substring substitutions to perform. If omitted, the default value is –1, means all possible substitutions.

compare - Optional. The kind of comparison to use can be text or binary compare.

Example: Chapter 7.23 - Replace_Examp.txt

Sub Replace_Examp()

Dim Word As String
Word = "Foundation day"

MsgBox Replace(Word, "da", "ab")
MsgBox Replace(Word, "da", "ab", 7)
MsgBox Replace(Word, "da", "ab", 1, 1)

End Sub

In this macro, we have declared word as string and assigned the text Foundation day. Now first message box we will get the answer **Founabtion aby** as it will replace all the occurrence of da with ab.

Second message box will return **tion aby** as the seach starts from the seventh place mentioned in the third parameter and then replace the occurrence of characters da.

Third message box we will return **Founabtion day** as we have given the fourth parameter to search and replace only the first occurance of **da**. Third parameter is where the search starts, here we have given one, so search starts from the first character of the text itself.

Space

This function creates a string consisting of a specified number of spaces.

Syntax:

Space(number)

Parameters:

number - The number of spaces to be returned.

Sub Space_Examp()

Dim SpaceString As String
SpaceString = "Hello" & Space(10) & "World"

MsgBox SpaceString

End Sub

Here we have given 10 as the parameter to the function Space in between the words Hello and World. So this will provide ten spaces automatically between the words Hello and World. Otherwise, we have to manually type the ten spaces like this "Hello   World". This function will be very useful if you want to dynamically put a space based on a condition.

StrComp

This function compares two strings and returns an integer representing the result of the comparison.

Syntax:

StrComp(string1, string2[, compare])

Parameters:

string1 – first text

string2 – second text.

compare - optional. Specifies the type of string comparison. If compare is omitted, the Option Compare setting determines the type of comparison text or binary.

Option Compare statement can be put in a module before any procedures are written.

The Option Compare statement specifies the string comparison method (Binary, Text, or Database) for a module.

Used at module level to declare the default comparison method to use when string data is compared.

Option Compare Binary string comparisons is based on a sort order derived from the internal binary representations of the characters. A typical binary sort order is shown in the following example.

A < B < E < Z < a < b < e < z < À < Ê < Ø < à < ê < ø

Points to Note:

If string1 is equal to string2, the StrComp function will return 0.

If string1 is less than string2, the StrComp function will return -1.

If string1 is greater than string2, the StrComp function will return 1.

If either string1 or string2 is NULL, the StrComp function will return NULL.

Example: Chapter 7.25 - StringComp_Examp.txt

Sub StringComp_Examp()

MsgBox StrComp("abc", "ABC", vbTextCompare)

MsgBox StrComp("abc", "ABC", vbBinaryCompare)

MsgBox StrComp("ABC", "ABC")

MsgBox StrComp("ABC", "abc")

End Sub

First, we use a Text Compare to compare abc with ABC. Since both the text is same, we will get the answer 0. In the second we use the Binary comparing and we will get 1 as string 1 is greater than string2. Third one we didn't use the third parameter so it will compare using Binary the default one. Fourth one also we have not specified the third parameter so it will use binary. Since string1 is less than string2, we will get the answer -1.

StrConv

This function converts a string into a specified format.

Syntax:

StrConv(String, Conversion, [LocaleID])

Parameters:

String - The string to be converted.

Conversion - specifying the type of conversion that is to be made. This can be any of the following values:

vbUpperCase - Convert to upper case characters.
vbLowerCase - Convert to lower case characters.
vbProperCase - Convert the first character of every word to upper case and all other characters to lower case.

vbWide - Convert narrow (single-byte) characters to wide (double-byte) characters (applies to East Asia locales only).

vbNarrow - Convert wide (double-byte) characters to narrow (single-byte) characters (applies to East Asia locales only).

vbKatakana - Convert Hiragana characters to Katakana characters (applies to Japan only).

vbHiragana - Convert Katakana characters to Hiragana characters (applies to Japan only).

vbUnicode - Convert to Unicode using the default code page of the system (not available on the Macintosh).

vbFromUnicode - Convert from Unicode to the default code page of the system (not available on the Macintosh).

[LocaleID] - An optional argument, specifying the LocaleID.

If omitted, the [LCID] argument uses the system LocaleID. You can find out more about this on Microsoft website.

Example: Chapter 7.26 - StrConv_Examp.txt

```
Sub StrConv_Examp()

    Dim MyString As String
    Dim Result As String

    MyString = "this is mine"
    Result = StrConv(MyString, vbUpperCase)
    MsgBox Result

    MyString = "THIS IS MINE"
    Result = StrConv(MyString, vbLowerCase)
    MsgBox Result

    MyString = "THIS IS MINE"
    Result = StrConv(MyString, vbProperCase)
    MsgBox Result

End Sub
```

In this example the string **this is mine** is converted to first uppercase, then the string **THIS IS MINE** IS converted to lowercase. Then last **THIS IS MINE** is converted to proper case.

StrReverse

This function reverses a supplied string.

Syntax:

StrReverse(expression)

Parameters:

expression – text to reverse.

Example: Chapter 7.27 - StrReverse_Examp.txt

Sub StrReverse_Examp()

Dim MyString As String
MyString = "Hello World"

MyString = StrReverse(MyString)
MsgBox MyString

End Sub

In this example, we have declared the MyString as datatype string and then assigned the text Hello World. Then we used the function StrReverse to reverse the text. A message box will return **dlroW olleH.**

Useful VBA File Management Functions

Dir

This will return the first file or directory name that matches a specified pattern and attributes. If you want to retrieve the subsequent file or directory name, then call the Dir function without any arguments.

Syntax:

Dir[(pathname[, attributes])]

Parameters:

Both the parameters are optional.

Pathname - String expression that specifies a file name - may include directory or folder, and drive. A zero-length string ("") is returned if pathname is not found.

Attributes - Constant or numeric expression, whose sum specifies file attributes. If omitted, returns files that match pathname but have no attributes.

The attributes argument are:

vbNormal 0 (Default) Specifies files with no attributes.

vbReadOnly 1 Specifies read-only files in addition to files with no attributes.

vbHidden 2 Specifies hidden files in addition to files with no attributes.

VbSystem 4 Specifies system files in addition to files with no attributes. Not available on the Macintosh.

vbVolume 8 Specifies volume label; if any other attributed is specified, vbVolume is ignored. Not available on the Macintosh.

vbDirectory 16 Specifies directories or folders in addition to files with no attributes.

vbAlias 64 Specified file name is an alias. Available only on the Macintosh.

Dir supports the use of multiple characters (*) and single character (?) wildcards to specify multiple files.

Example: Chapter 7.28 - Dir_Examp.txt

Sub Dir_Examp()

Dim MyDir As String

MyDir = ("E:\HI\")

MsgBox Dir(MyDir)

MsgBox Dir()

End Sub

For this example to work first you create a folder under E drive called **HI (** if there is no E drive then create in another one and change the MyDir path to your drive letter**).** Then you create two text files in this folder and run this macro. It will display the file names under the folder HI. Here, we have stored the path in the MyDir string variable and assigned the path to the Dir function. Since there are two files in the directory, we have used the Dir function two times. First time with the path and the next time without the path(the path is known from the first calling of Dir function). You will get two file names inside the folder as message box.

But the above program is not perfect; what if there are more than two files. We have mentioned only two files message boxes so that it will display only two file names. So to bypass that we will use a loop like this.

Example: Chapter 7.29 - Dir_Examp1.txt

Sub Dir_Examp1()

Dim MyDir As String, Path As String

MyDir = ("E:\HI\")
Path = Dir(MyDir)

```
Do Until Path = vbNullString
MsgBox Path
Path = Dir()
Loop


End Sub
```

Here we have declared two string variables MyDir and Path and stored the path in MyDir. Then we used the Dir function to store the first file name in the path variable. Now we used a Do until loop to loop through all the files. Inside the Do loop, the message box will display the first file name and then again we call the Dir function and assign it to the path variable. Now the loop checks whether the variable path contains anything. Since we have assigned the Dir() function it contains the second file name and we will get the second file name. Like that it loops through the entire files and display all files. If no files are available, it will be null and Do loop will exit.

Now we will change the above example slightly and use an attribute. For that, you add a new folder to the HI directory. We are going to list the file names and directory names.

Example: Chapter 7.30 - Dir_Examp2.txt

```
Sub Dir_Examp2()

Dim MyDir As String, Path As String

MyDir = ("E:\HI\")
Path = Dir(MyDir, vbDirectory)

Do Until Path = vbNullString
MsgBox Path
Path = Dir()
Loop

End Sub
```

Now, this program will display all the directories and files. Like this, you can use other attributes also to check any hidden files, read only files, system files, etc. For that, you have to change the attribute argument.

Dir function can be used to check whether a file exists. This is particularly useful when you want to execute some codes if a particular file exists. It can be done with the combination of IF and Len function. Let's go through an example.

Example: Chapter 7.31 - Dir_Examp3.txt

```
Sub Dir_Examp3()

Dim MyFile As String
```

```vba
MyFile = ("E:\HI\as.txt")

If (Len(Dir(MyFile))) = 0 Then

MsgBox "File doesn't exist"

' you can write the code here

Else

MsgBox "File Exists"

End If

End Sub
```

First, create the file as.txt under HI folder. Here we are using the Len function to check the length of the string returned from Dir function. And If the length is zero, means the file is not available we will get the Message box 'File doesn't exist' else we will get the message File Exists. Here we will get the answer File Exists.

Here if the file does not exist, you can write the code for what has to be done.

You can also use wildcards also with Dir function. * for multiple characters including zero length and ? for a single character.

For example Dir("C:\WelcomeHome.txt") matches **WelcomeHome.txt.**

Dir("C:\Welcome*Home.txt") matches **WelcomeHome.txt** or **WelcometoHome.txt** or **Welcome_home.txt.**

Dir("C:\?elcomeHome.txt") matches **WelcomeHome.txt** or **LelcomeHome.txt** or **HelcomeHome.txt.**

Close and Open Method

The Close and Open Method in Excel VBA can be used to close and open workbooks. Remember, the Workbooks collection contains all the Workbook objects that are currently open.

The code line below closes sales.xls if it is opened

Workbooks("sales.xls").Close

The code line below closes the first opened/created workbook.

Workbooks(1).Close

The code line below closes the active workbook.

ActiveWorkbook.Close

The code line below closes all workbooks that are currently open.

Workbooks.Close

The code line below opens sales.xls.

Workbooks.Open ("sales.xls")

Note: You can only open sales.xls without specifying the file's path if it's stored in your default file location. The default file location is the folder you see when you open or save a file.

GetOpenFilename Method

This method of the Application object is used to display the standard open Dialog box and without actually opening the file.

Syntax:

expression .GetOpenFilename(FileFilter, FilterIndex, Title, ButtonText, MultiSelect)

expression A variable that represents an Application object.

Parameters:

All these parameters are optional.

FileFilter –This determines the types of files that will be displayed in the Files Of Type drop-down list

FilterIndex –This specifies which file filter is the default. Not required if there is only one filter provided.

Title - Specifies the title of the dialog box. If this argument is omitted, the title is "Open."

ButtonText – Macintosh only.

MultiSelect – True to allow multiple file names to be selected. False to allow only one file name to be selected. The default value is False.

Example: Chapter 7.32 - GetOpen_Examp.txt

Sub GetOpen_Examp()

Dim TheFile As String

TheFile = Application.GetOpenFilename()

Workbooks.Open (TheFile)

End Sub

This macro will open up a standard open dialogue box and you can select the file to open.

Here is another example.

Example: Chapter 7.33 - GetOpen_Examp1.txt

Sub GetOpen_Examp1()

Dim FileFilter As String
Dim FiletoOpen As Variant

FileFilter = "Excel Files,*.xlsx," & "Text Files ,*.txt, " & "All Files ,*.*"

FiletoOpen = Application.GetOpenFilename(FileFilter:=FileFilter, _
           FilterIndex:=1, _
           Title:="Open a New or an Old File", _
           MultiSelect:=False)

If FiletoOpen = False Then
MsgBox "You have clicked Cancel."
End If

End Sub

We have declared two variables FileFilter and FiletoOpen. FileFilter holds the filter to show when the open dialogue box is shown. Then we are storing the return value of the GetOpenFilename in FiletoOpen variable. Then in the GetOpenFilename, we give the first parameter the string variable FileFilter we have declared. Second, we give the FilterIndex as 1 so it will show the first filter with only *.xlsx files which you have mentioned in the FileFilter variable. If you want to make the second one as the default one you change it to 2 to get *.txt as default. Then you give third argument the Title **Open a New or an Old File** and fourth one MultiSelect option is set to False so you cannot select multiple files.

If you have canceled the open dialogue box, we will get false and we are checking the value false and showing a message box You have clicked Cancel.

Worksheet Functions in VBA

You can use most of the Excel functions in VBA by clubbing it with WorksheetFunction object. The WorksheetFunction object contained in the Application object holds all the worksheet functions that you can call from your VBA procedures.

To use a worksheet function in a VBA statement, just precede the function name with Application.WorksheetFunction.

For example, if you want to find an average of A1:A10. You can use it like this,

 MsgBox Application.WorksheetFunction.Average(Range("A1:A10")) or use **WorksheetFunction.Average(Range("A1:A10"))**

Another way if you want to insert a formula into the cell B2 you can do it like this.

Range("B2").Value = "=AVERAGE(A1:A10)"

Or if you want to enter the value into B1:B10 cell you can change it like this.

Range("B1:B10").Value = "=AVERAGE(A1:A10)"

Chapter 8

Operators in Excel VBA

If you add 4 + 10 you will get 14. Here, 4 and 10 are called operands and + is called operator. VBA supports following types of operators. VBA supports all the standard operations which Excel has.

Arithmetic Operators

If A is 4 and B is 10, then.

+   Adds the two operands, A + B will give 14

-        Subtracts the second operand from the first, A - B will give -6

*   Multiplies both the operands, A * B will give 40

/   Divides the numerator by the denominator, B / A will give 2.5

^   Exponentiation operator, B ^ A will give 10000

mod   Modulus, divides a number and returns the reminder, B mod A will give 2.

Comparison Operators

If A is 4 and B is 10, then.

= - Checks if the value of the two operands is equal. If yes, then the condition is true, Here (A = B) is False.

<> - Checks if the value of the two operands is not equal. If the values are not equal, then the condition is true. Here (A <> B) is True.

> - Checks if the value of the left operand is greater than the value of the right operand. If yes, then the condition is true. Here (A > B) is False.

< - Checks if the value of the left operand is less than the value of the right operand. If yes, then the condition is true. Here (A < B) is True.

\>= - Checks if the value of the left operand is greater than or equal to the value of the right operand. If yes, then the condition is true. Here (A >= B) is False.

<= - Checks if the value of the left operand is less than or equal to the value of the right operand. If yes, then the condition is true. Here (A <= B) is True.

Logical (or Relational) Operators

If A is 4 and B is 10, then.

AND - Logical AND operator. If both the conditions are True, then the Expression is true. Here A<>0 AND B<>0 then it is True.

OR - Logical OR Operator. If any of the two conditions are True, then the condition is true. Here A<>0 OR B<>0 is True.

NOT - Logical NOT Operator. Used to reverse the logical state of its operand. If a condition is true, then Logical NOT operator will make false. Here NOT(A<>0 OR B<>0) is false.

XOR - Logical Exclusion. It is the combination of NOT and OR Operator. If one, and only one, of the expressions evaluates to be True, the result is True. Here (A<>0 XOR B<>0) is false.

Concatenation Operators

Here variable A holds 5 and variable B holds 10 then

+ - Adds two Values as numeric Variable. A + B will give 15.

& - Concatenates two Values. A & B will give 510

Assume variable A = "Hello" and variable B = "Wold", then

+ - Concatenates two Values   A + B will give HelloWorld

& - Concatenates two Values   A & B will give HelloWorld

Concatenation Operators can be used for both numbers and strings. The output will differ if the variables hold numeric value or string value.

Operator Operation Order of Precedence

^ -- Exponentiation - Order of Precedence 1

* -- and / Multiplication and division - Order of Precedence 2

+ and - -- Addition and subtraction Order of Precedence - 3

& -- Concatenation Order of Precedence 4

=, <, >, <=, >=, <> -- Comparison - Order of Precedence 5

Example: Chapter 8.1 - Operator_Examp.txt

```
Sub Operator_Examp()

  Dim x As Integer, y As Integer
  x = 10
  y = 0

  If x <> 0 And y <> 0 Then
    MsgBox ("AND Operator Result is : True")
  Else
    MsgBox ("AND Operator Result is : False")
  End If

  If x <> 0 Or y <> 0 Then
    MsgBox ("OR Operator Result is : True")
  Else
    MsgBox ("OR Operator Result is : False")
  End If

  If Not (x <> 0 Or y <> 0) Then
    MsgBox ("NOT Operator Result is : True")
  Else
    MsgBox ("NOT Operator Result is : False")
  End If

End Sub
```

When you run this program, you will get the result like this.

AND Operator Result is: False

OR Operator Result is: True

NOT Operator Result is: False

AND Operator Result is: False - Value of x is not equal to 0, but the value of y is equal to zero. But for AND operator both the conditions should be satisfied hence it will raise false.

AND Operator Result is: False – OR operator wants any of the condition to be true. Here the X is not equal to zero. So you will get the result as True.

NOT Operator Result is: False – If you put a not operator in the beginning, it will reverse what is derived if it is false it will change to true and true to false.

Chapter 9

Controlling Program Flow and Making Decisions

VBA usually executes from first line of code to the last line in an orderly manner. This is called Structured programming. Macros that you record always work like this. Most of the simple programs can be written like this.

The power and flexibility of VBA is the ability to change this order of execution with control statements and loops. You can skip over some statements, execute some statements multiple times, and make test conditions to determine what the procedure does next.

How we are doing it is discussed in detail in this chapter.

Decisions

If-Then

This is most commonly used decision-making construct. IF-Then structure will execute the statements written if it is true. For example, you want to check if a cell contains the number 5. If this is true, then you can write your statement.

Syntax:

IF condition **Then** true_instructions [**Else** false_instructions]

Else part is optional and you can use it as per your requirement.

The piece of code between the IF and the Then keywords is called the condition. A condition is a statement that evaluates to true or false. They are mostly used with Loops and IF statements. When you create a condition you use signs like **>, <, <>, >=, <=, =.**

The following are examples of conditions.

x < 7 - This is true when x is less than 7

x <= 7 - This is true when x is less than or equal to 7

x > 7 - This is true when x is greater than 7

x >= 7 - This is true when x is greater than or equal to 7

x = 7 - This is true when x is equal to 7

x <> 7 - This is true when x does not equal 7

x > 7 And x < 10 - This is true when x is greater than 7 AND x is less than 10

x = 2 Or x >10 - This is true when x is equal to 2 OR x is greater than 10

Range("A1") = "John" - This is true when Cell A1 contains text "John"

Range("A1") <> "John" - This is true when Cell A1 does not contain text "John"

We will look into an example.

Example: Chapter 9.1 - If_Example1.txt

Sub If_Example1()

Dim X As Integer
X = 5

If X = 5 Then MsgBox "X is " & X

End Sub

Here we have declared the variable X and assigned the number to it. Then we have used the IF condition to check the variable is 5. If it is 5, we are calling the Msgbox function to display the result.

In the above example, I have written the IF condition in a single line. You can split the IF condition to multiple lines like this in the below example. If you are splitting the IF condition to multiple lines then you have to use the keywords Then and End if.

Example: Chapter 9.2 - If_Example2.txt

Sub If_Example2()

Dim X As Integer
X = 5

If X = 5 Then
MsgBox "X is " & X
End If

End Sub

In this case, you have to put an **End If** where you think the IF condition ends. Otherwise, the program will throw an error, Block If without End If. If you are not writing the IF condition in a single line then we must use **Then** keyword and **End If**. After the Then keyword we can write the action to be taken and End if is mentioned to denote the end of IF condition.

Here is another example written for you to understand.

Example: Chapter 9.3 - If_Example3.txt

Sub IF_Example3()

Dim num As Integer

num = WorksheetFunction.RandBetween(5, 7)

If num = 5 Then MsgBox "Num is " & num
If num = 6 Then MsgBox "Num is " & num
If num = 7 Then MsgBox "Num is " & num

End Sub

Here we have used three IF conditions. First, we have made use of Excels built-in function Randbetween to generate the numbers between 5 to 7 randomly and store it in the variable num. After that, we checked whether num has 5 or 6 or 7 using IF and then displays the num variable value using Message box function. You can run this procedure two-three times to see the results.

In this program all the IF conditions will get tested even if you get the answer in the first line itself.

If-Then-Else

Example: Chapter 9.4 - IF_Example4.txt

Sub IF_Example4()

Dim num As Integer

num = WorksheetFunction.RandBetween(5, 6)

If num = 5 Then
MsgBox "Num is " & num
Else
MsgBox "Num is " & num
End If

End Sub

You can write the IF condition using IF, Then and Else. You have to mention the condition after the IF and the keyword Then after that. So if the condition is true, you can display a message box and if the condition is false, you can mention the same in the Else part and then close the IF condition with End if.

ElseIf

It is not mandatory to use the Else block with every IF statement. The syntax is given below.

IF condition_1 THEN

 'Instructions inside First IF Block

ELSEIF condition_2 Then

 'Instructions inside ELSEIF Block

...

ELSEIF condition_n Then

 'Instructions inside nth ELSEIF Block

ELSE 'Instructions inside Else Block

END IF

Given below is another example where I'm rewriting the previous example using the optional Else if.

Example: Chapter 9.5 - IF_Example5.txt

Sub IF_Example5()

Dim num As Integer

num = WorksheetFunction.RandBetween(5, 7)

If num = 5 Then
MsgBox "Num is " & num

ElseIf num = 6 Then
MsgBox "Num is " & num

Else
MsgBox "Num is " & num

End If

End Sub

Here first we have evaluated whether the num is 5 if it is not 5 it will go to the elseif block and if that is also not true then it will go to the Else section.

The conditions along with the IF Statements will be evaluated sequentially. So if the IF condition is true then instruction inside the IF block will get executed and rest of the blocks will be skipped. It is different from the previous example where all the If's are evaluated. In other words, only one block will get executed which evaluates to true in sequential order.

Remember that out of IF, ELSEIF's and ELSE code blocks; only a single code block will be executed at a time based on the condition.

In the example given below, we are checking whether the entered number is positive or negative. Since we have declared the variable number as Integer, if we enter any other characters it will throw up an error and for catching that error I have put a Go To statement. In the Error part we have mentioned to display a message box **Please enter a positive or negative number.** GoTo is explained in depth in the coming sections.

Example: Chapter 9.6 - IF_Example6.txt

```
Sub IF_Example6 ()

On Error GoTo ErrorPart

Dim number As Integer

number = InputBox("Enter the number: ")

If number < 0 Then
MsgBox "Entered number is Negative!"

Else
MsgBox "Entered number is Positive!"

End If

Exit Sub

ErrorPart:
MsgBox "Please enter a positive or negative number"

End Sub
```

Using IF statement with And & Or operators

You can check multiple conditions with logical operators inside a single IF statement. There are many logical operators in VBA like And, Or, Not, and Xor but in most cases, we only deal with the first three.

All the operators mentioned above are binary (i.e., they accept at least two operands) except NOT. NOT is unary because it takes a single operand.

139

For And operator both the conditions should be correct to return True and for OR any of the Condition should be true.

Let us look into an example which uses both IF condition and the AND operator.

Example: Chapter 9.7 - IF_Example7.txt

```
Sub IF_Example7()

On Error GoTo ErrorPart

Dim Drinks1 As String, Drinks2 As String

Drinks1 = InputBox("You like Coffee or Tea?")
Drinks2 = InputBox("You like Juice or Softdrink?")

If LCase(Drinks1) = "coffee" And LCase(Drinks2) = "juice" Then
MsgBox "I too like these"

Else
MsgBox "I don't like these"

End If

Exit Sub

ErrorPart: MsgBox "Unexpected error, Please contact system administrator"

End Sub
```

Here we are checking whether the Input we have received is Coffee and Juice. We have put an AND operator in the IF condition so both the inputs should be matching, it must be Coffee and Juice. If both inputs are matching IF condition becomes true and you will get the answer I too like the same. Else if it is false it will execute the Else part I don't like these.

I have used LCase in the IF condition to convert the Inputbox variable to lower case. User may enter value in upper case or lower case or mixed case. So for matching purpose we are converting it to lower case and matching.

Let us look into an example which used both IF condition and the OR operator.

Example: Chapter 9.8 - IF_Example8.txt

```
Sub IF_Example8 ()

On Error GoTo ErrorPart

Dim Drinks As String

Drinks = InputBox("You like Coffee or Tea?")
```

If LCase(Drinks) = "coffee" Or LCase(Drinks) = "tea" Then

MsgBox "I too like the same."

Else: MsgBox "I don't like that"

End If

Exit Sub

ErrorPart: MsgBox "Unexpected error, Please contact system administrator"

End Sub

In this example, we are checking whether the Input we have received is either Tea or Coffee. We have put an OR operator in the IF condition so if the input is either Coffee or Tea you will get the answer **I too like the same.**

Another example using IF condition for finding out the grades of the students. In this example, if you enter the score in the Inputbox you will get the grade. Grades criteria are like this.

85 to 100 is Grade A
75 to 84 is Grade B
65 to 74 is Grade C
55 to 64 is Grade D
45 to 54 is Grade E
Less than 45 is Fail

Here we have used the And operator along with the IF operator

Example: Chapter 9.9 - IF_Example9.txt

Sub IF_Example9()

On Error GoTo ErrorPart

Dim Score As Integer
Score = InputBox("Enter your Score: ")

If Score <= 100 And Score >= 85 Then
MsgBox "Grade A"

ElseIf Score < 85 And Score >= 75 Then
MsgBox "Grade B"

ElseIf Score < 75 And Score >= 65 Then
MsgBox "Grade C"

ElseIf Score < 65 And Score >= 55 Then

MsgBox "Grade D"

ElseIf Score < 55 And Score >= 45 Then
MsgBox "Grade E"

ElseIf Score < 45 Then
MsgBox "You are Failed"

End If

Exit Sub

ErrorPart:
MsgBox "Error Please contact system administrator"

End Sub

Points to Note: It is always good to use Select Case statements instead of writing multiple ELSEIF statements like in the above example. Select Case statements execute faster and look cleaner than IF THEN ELSE. We will go through Select case shortly.

Select Case

Select Case Statement is one of the best methods for checking multiple conditions. You don't need multiple IF Statements which can make Excel VBA code very hard to read and decipher. Select Case is very similar to the IF statement in its functionality, however, Select case is more flexible.

Syntax:

Select Case < Expression to test>

   Case condition_1
   result_1

  Case condition_2
   result_2

  ...

  Case condition_n
   result_n

  Case Else
   result_else

End Select

Parameters:

test_expression - a string or numeric value. It is the value that you are comparing to the list of conditions. (ie: condition_1, condition_2, ... condition_n)

condition_1, ... condition_n - conditions that are evaluated in the order listed. Once a condition is found to be true, it will execute the corresponding code and not evaluate the conditions any further.

result_1, ... result_n - the code that is executed once a condition is found to be true.

Let's look at some examples and explore how to use the CASE statement in Excel VBA code.

Example: Chapter 9.10 - SelectCase_Examp1.txt

```
Sub SelectCase_Examp1()

Dim CellValue As Long
CellValue = Range("A1").Value

Select Case CellValue

Case 100
Range("B1").Value = 50

Case 200
Range("B1").Value = 40

Case 300
Range("B1").Value = 30

Case 400
Range("B1").Value = 20

Case 500
Range("B1").Value = 10

Case Else
Range("B1").Value = 0

End Select

End Sub
```

In this example first we have declared a variable CellValue as long to hold the numbers. Second we have assigned the cell value of A1 to this variable.

Then we have assigned that to the Select Case statement to test by using Select Case CellValue. After that CellValues value is checked against each value mentioned in the five cases. For that first, we mentioned the Case followed by the condition to check. So here First condition we have given is 100. So if A1 cell contains 100 the first condition becomes true then B1 cell value will become 50. If the A1 cell value is 200, second case condition will be true and you will get the answer 40.

If all the five conditions are not met, you can put a Case Else and write the statement you want.

In the above example, we have checked all the individual cases. What if we want to perform some action if the Range A1 is equal to any one of the Values 100,200,300,400, 500. If this is the case, we could use Select case like this in the example given below.

Example: Chapter 9.11 - SelectCase_Examp2.txt

```
Sub SelectCase_Examp2()

Dim CellValue As Long

CellValue = Range("A1").Value

Select Case CellValue

Case 100, 200, 300, 400, 500
Range("B1").Value = 50

Case Else
Range("B1").Value = 0

End Select

End Sub
```


Another example.

Now if you only want to have some action if the range(s) are between two numbers. Then you can rewrite like this.

Example: Chapter 9.12 - SelectCase_Examp3.txt

```
Sub SelectCase_Examp3()

Dim CellValue As Long
CellValue = Range("A1").Value

Select Case CellValue

Case 100 To 200
Range("B1").Value = 50

Case 201 To 300
Range("B1").Value = 40

Case 301 To 400
```

```vba
Range("B1").Value = 30

Case 401 To 500
Range("B1").Value = 20

Case Else
Range("B1").Value = 0

End Select

End Sub
```

Now, what about if we needed to check if cell A1 was not only between 100 and 500 but also between 900 and 1200, 2500 and 2900. You can change Select Case like this example.

Example: Chapter 9.13 - SelectCase_Examp4.txt

```vba
Sub SelectCase_Examp4()

Dim CellValue As Long

CellValue = Range("A1").Value

Select Case CellValue

Case 100 To 500, 900 To 1200, 2500 To 2900
Range("B1").Value = 50

Case Else
Range("B1").Value = 0

End Select

End Sub
```

Now we will rewrite the Grade_Calculation_selectcase example written in IF condition before with the select case. It will be easy.

Example: Chapter 9.14 - SelectCase_Examp5.txt

```vba
Sub SelectCase_Examp5 ()

On Error GoTo ErrorPart

Dim Score As Integer
Score = InputBox("Enter your Score: ")

Select Case Score

    Case 85 to 100
    MsgBox "Grade A"
```

145

```vba
    Case 75 to 84
    MsgBox "Grade B"

    Case 65 to 74
    MsgBox "Grade C"

    Case 55 to 64
    MsgBox "Grade D"

    Case 45 to 54
    MsgBox "Grade E"

    Case Else
    MsgBox "Failed"

    End Select

Exit Sub

ErrorPart:
MsgBox "Error Please contact system administrator"

End Sub
```

Using GOTO and Labels

GoTo statement Jumps to a particular statement from the middle of the program to a label you specify (a text string followed by a colon, or a number with no colon). VBA procedure can have any number of labels but Go To statement cannot go beyond the current procedure.

We will go through an example.

Example: Chapter 9.15 - Goto_Examp.txt

```vba
Sub Goto_Examp()

Dim Welcome As String
Welcome = InputBox("Enter the word, hi")

If Welcome <> "hi" Then GoTo Errorpart

MsgBox "Correct answer"

Exit Sub

Errorpart: MsgBox ("You have not entered the word hi")

End Sub
```

Here we have declared a Welcome variable as string datatype. Data retrieved from the Inputbox is assigned to the Welcome. After that we are checking the entered value is hi. If it is not hi, it will go directly to the label mentioned at the end GoTo. Here in the label, we have put a message box showing, You have not entered the word hi.

If you have entered the word hi in the input box, the IF condition will become false. Then you will get a message box showing the text **Correct Answer**. Since you don't have to go to the label part, you are putting an Exit sub to exit the procedure. Without Exit sub the label part will also get executed.

Instead of the mentioning the label Errorpart: you can put a number without colon.

Although it is easy to put a Go To statement here and there it is not a good programming practice. Program should execute from top to bottom in an orderly manner. Other wise it will be difficult to maintain and logic of the program will be confusing. So use Go To sparingly. You only need this for error handling only.

Loops

Loops are used to repeat a block of code as many times you specify or until a given condition remains true or a specific value is reached. Once the loop is completed the next section of code is executed.

There are three basic kinds of VBA Loops subdivided into six loops as below.

1. For Loops.

2. Do While Loops.

3. Do Until Loops.

1. The For Loop

    a. The For … Next Statements

    b. The For Each … Next Statements

a. FOR...NEXT

The For … Next Loop repeats a block of code a specific number of times.

Syntax:

For counter_variable = start_value To end_value [Step stepcount]

Your code

Next counter_variable

We will go through an example for you to understand.

Example: Chapter 9.16 - ForNext_Examp1.txt

Sub ForNext_Examp1()

Dim iTotal As Integer
Dim iCounter As Integer

For iCounter = 1 To 5
        iTotal = iCounter + iTotal
Next iCounter

MsgBox iTotal

End Sub

Here I have declared two variables iTotal and iCounter as integer. The start_value of the iCounter is 1, and its end_value is 5. You can mention the "Step" keyword (it is optional) if you want. This is a numeric value by which the counter is incremented each time the loop is run. The default step value is 1, so you don't have to specify it here.

The Next statement increments the icounter by one and returns to the For statement. It repeats the block of code till the icounter value reaches the end value of 5. Once the icounter becomes 6 the loop will stop and next line of code will execute. The block of code which is repeated in this loop is: **"iTotal = iCounter + iTotal".**

So once the loops starts, the iCounter variable will be 1 and this will be added to the iTotal again and again when the loop runs. So when the first loop completes iTotal will have the value 1. Second time the loop runs counter value will be 2 and 2 will be added to iTotal value. So you will get the value 3 stored in the iTotal. This goes on till the counter reaches five.

You will get the answer 15. You can add a Debug.Print statement inside the loop after this code iTotal = iCounter + iTotal (Debug.Print iTotal) to see the iTotal value in the immediate window when the loop runs. You can use the shortcut Ctrl + G to view the Immediate window.

Now we will go through an example with step argument to see what happens.

Example: Chapter 9.17 - ForNext_Examp2.txt

Sub ForNext_Examp2()

Dim iTotal As Integer
Dim iCounter As Integer

For iCounter = 1 To 5 Step 2
iTotal = iCounter + iTotal

Next iCounter

MsgBox iTotal

End Sub

Since you added the step as 2, loop will jump two steps. iCounter variable starts from 1 and in the second loop iCounter will have the value 3, i.e., 1+2. In the third loop, iCounter value will be 3+2 = 5. There won't be any fourth loop as the next loop value is 7 which exceed the permitted loop range 5.

Now we will go through an example with step argument negative and see what happens.

Example: Chapter 9.18 - ForNext_Examp3.txt

Sub ForNext_Examp3()

Dim iTotal As Integer
Dim iCounter As Integer

For iCounter = 5 To 1 Step -1
iTotal = iCounter + iTotal
Next iCounter

MsgBox iTotal

End Sub

Here the loop starts from higher number 5 to the lowest number 1 because we have specified the step value as -1. We will get the answer 15. You can change the step value to suite your requirement.

A For-Next example with an Exit For statement

Example: Chapter 9.19 - ForNext_Examp4.txt

Sub ForNext_Examp4()

Dim iTotal As Integer
Dim iCounter As Integer

For iCounter = 1 To 5
iTotal = iCounter + iTotal
If iCounter = 4 Then Exit For
Next iCounter

MsgBox iTotal

End Sub

In this example, we have used an IF condition inside the counter. So if the iCounter reaches the value 4 it will exit the For loop. For exiting the For loop we have used the statement Exit For.

If you place the IF condition before the code **iTotal = iCounter + iTotal**, counter value 4 will not get added to the iTotal.

Try this for yourself and see what happens.

Here is another example which writes the values of the iCounter from 1 to 5 to the cells A1 to A5.

Example: Chapter 9.20 - ForNext_Examp5.txt

Sub ForNext_Examp5()

Dim iCounter As Integer
For iCounter = 1 To 5

ActiveSheet.Cells(iCounter, 1).Value = iCounter
Next iCounter

End Sub

Here we have used the Application objects cell property to assign the values. Application object has the ActiveSheet property. So it will use the active excel sheet to write the values. Cells property has two parameters, first one is row number and second one is column number. Since we want all the values to be entered in A column, we have given the variable iCounter as row number. So it will change the row number each time the loop runs.

If you want to place the values column wise place the iCounter variable as second parameter.

Single Loop

You can use a single loop to loop through a one-dimensional range of cells.

Example: Chapter 9.21 - ForNext_Examp6.txt

Sub ForNext_Examp6()

Dim i As Integer

For i = 1 To 6
  Application.Cells(i, 1).Value = 50
Next i

End Sub

This macro will write the value 50 from cell A1 to A6. This loop will run six times as we have mentioned the value starts from 1 to 6. Each time the loop is executed i variable inside the Cells property changes. Cells properties first argument is row number and the second one is column number.

So each time the row changes inside the loop and the value 50 will get updated in the particular cell.

Instead of writing Application.cells you can start with Cells. Why I have mentioned Application is to make it clear that that the cells property belongs to the Application Object.

Double Loop

You can use a double loop to loop through a two-dimensional range of cells.

Example: Chapter 9.22 - ForNext_Examp7.txt

```
Sub ForNext_Examp7()

Dim i As Integer, j As Integer

For i = 1 To 6

   For j = 1 To 2
      Cells(i, j).Value = 50
   Next j

Next i

End Sub
```

Here both the row number and column number is derived from i and j variables of the For Next loop. This type of loop is very useful to fill the ranges.

Triple Loop

You can use a triple loop to loop through two-dimensional ranges on multiple Excel worksheets.

Example: Chapter 9.23 - ForNext_Examp8.txt

```
Sub ForNext_Examp8()

Dim c As Integer, i As Integer, j As Integer

For c = 1 To 3

   For i = 1 To 6

      For j = 1 To 2

         Worksheets(c).Cells(i, j).Value = 50

      Next j

   Next i

Next c

End Sub
```

Before running this macro, check there are three sheets in the Excel workbook.

The only change compared to the code for the double loop is that we have added one more loop and added Worksheets(c) in front of Cells. So the c variable loops through the three sheets.

b. For Each-Next constructs or For Each...Next Loop

Unlike the previous For Loop, For Each ... Next Loop repeats a block of code for each Object in a group. It repeats the execution of a block of code, for each element of a collection. The loop stops when all the elements in the collection have been covered, and execution moves to the section of code immediately following the Next statement.

The syntax of the For Each-Next construct is:

For Each element In collection

[instructions]

[Exit For]

[instructions]

Next [element]

We will go through the example.

Example: Chapter 9.24 - For_Each_Examp1.txt

```
Sub For_Each_Examp1()

    Dim Cell As Range

    For Each Cell In Selection
        Cell.Value = UCase(Cell.Value)
    Next Cell

End Sub
```

First, we have declared a variable cell to hold the Range Object. Next, we have put a For Each Next loop to go through the selection to change the selected cells to uppercase. Enter some small letters in the cells and select that before executing this macro. Here selection means the selected range of cells. This is a property of Application and returns a Range object if you have selected the cells.

This loops through each cell in the Range("A1:A20") and sets the background color of the cell to red in each cell.

Example: Chapter 9.25 - For_Each_Examp2.txt

Sub For_Each_Examp2()

Dim rCell As Range

For Each rCell In ActiveSheet.Range("A1:A20")
rCell.Interior.Color = RGB(255, 0, 0)
Next rCell

End Sub

Here, rCell is the Range Object variable, and the group or collection are the Cells in the Range("A1:A20"). The Interior.color property will set the color to red which is specified in the RGB.

You can get the RGB color from the Excel itself. Click the drop down arrow in Font color or Fill color Icon in Excel Home tab. Select More colors > Custom Tab. There you can see the RGB values which you can make use of.

You can also nest an IF statement within a For ... Each Loop like this.

Example: Chapter 9.26 - For_Each_Examp3.txt

Sub For_Each_Examp3()

Dim rCell As Range

For Each rCell In ActiveSheet.Range("A1:A20")

If rCell > 10 Then
rCell.Interior.Color = RGB(255, 0, 0)

Else
rCell.Interior.Color = RGB(255, 255, 0)

End If

Next rCell

End Sub

The code loops through each cell in the range A1:A20, and if cell value exceeds 10, background color of that cell is set as Red, else Yellow for values of 10 and less. Fill some values below ten and above ten in the range A1:A20 and run this macro.

You can also use Exit for in this loop if you want to exit the loop if a condition is met.

2. The Do While Loop

The Do While Loop repeats a block of code indefinitely while the specified condition is True, and stops when the condition turns False. There are two ways you can use this loop. Either the condition can be tested at the start or at the end of the Loop.

"The Do While ... Loop Statements" test the condition at the start, while "The Do ... Loop While Statements" test the condition at the end of the Loop. If the condition is tested at the start of the Loop and the condition is met, the block of code does not run even once. If the condition is tested at the end, the Loop runs at least once.

a. The Do While ... Loop Statements

Syntax:

 Do While [Condition]

[block of code]

Loop

Example: Chapter 9.27 - Do_While_Examp1.txt

```
Sub Do_While_Examp1()

Dim iCounter As Integer
Dim iTotal As Integer

iCounter = 5
iTotal = 0

Do While iCounter > 5
iTotal = iCounter + iTotal
iCounter = iCounter - 1
Loop

MsgBox iTotal

End Sub
```

Here we have declared two integer variables iCounter and iTotal. iCounter we have set the value as 5 as we have to loop five times. iTotal we have set the value as 0.

The condition iCounter > 5 is tested at the start and returns the value false because iCounter value is 5, not greater than 5. So the loop does not execute even once and you will get answer zero.

b. The Do ... Loop While Statements

Syntax:

Do

[block of code]

Loop While [Condition]

Example: Chapter 9.28 - Do_While_Examp2.txt

Sub Do_While_Examp2()

Dim iCounter As Integer
Dim iTotal As Integer
iCounter = 5
iTotal = 0

Do

iTotal = iCounter + iTotal

iCounter = iCounter - 1

Loop While iCounter > 5

MsgBox iTotal

End Sub

It is the same example, but we have placed While iCounter > 5 after the word loop. Now, this loop will execute at least once and the value of the iCounter will be reduced to 4. Since we have mentioned the While part at the end it will exit the loop as the iCounter is not greater than 5.

iTotal returns the value 5 because of one time execution.

The Exit Do Statement

You can exit the Do While Loop early, without completing the full cycle, by using the Exit Do statement. The Exit Do statement will immediately stop the execution of the existing loop and execute the section of code immediately following the Loop statement. And in the case of inner nested level, it will stop and execute the next outer nested level.

You can have any number of Exit Do statements in a loop. It is particularly useful in case you want to terminate the loop on reaching a certain value or satisfying a specific condition, or in case you want to terminate an endless loop at a certain point. It is similar to the Exit For statement used to exit the For Loop.

```
Sub ExitDo_Examp()

Dim iCounter As Integer

Do While iCounter < 11

iCounter = iCounter + 1

If iCounter = ActiveSheet.Range("A1") Then

Exit Do

End If

Loop

MsgBox iCounter

End Sub
```

Before executing the code put a value below 11 in the cell A1.

Here I have declared the iCounter variable as an integer. Then we have given the condition that iCounter must loop till it is less than 11. Inside the loop, iCounter value increaes by one each time the loop runs. After that, we have put an IF condition to check whether the iCounter value is equal to value in the cell A1. Once the value is equal, IF will execute the Exit Do statement to end the loop.

So if you have entered 5 in A1 cell the loop will iterate 5 times and then exit the loop and you will get the return value 5. If you have not put any value in A1 cell then loop will go through its full cycle and you will get the answer 11 mentioned in the Do loop Condition.

3. The Do Until Loop

The Do Until Loop repeats a block of code indefinitely until the condition is met and evaluates to True. The condition can be tested either at the start or at the end of the Loop. "The Do Until ... Loop Statements" test the condition at the start, while "The Do ... Loop Until Statements" test the condition at the end of the Loop.

If the condition is tested at the start of the Loop and the condition is met, the block of code does not run even once. If the condition is tested at the end, the Loop runs at least once.

a. The Do Until ... Loop Statements

Syntax:

Do Until [Condition]

[block of code]

Loop

Example: Chapter 9.30 - DoUntil_Examp1.txt

Sub DoUntil_Examp1()

Dim iCounter As Integer

  iCounter = 10

  Do Until iCounter > 15

    iCounter = iCounter + 1

    MsgBox ("The value of iCounter is : " & iCounter)

  Loop

End Sub

Here we have declared the iCounter variable as integer. Since we have put the condition to loop until iCounter is greater than 15 the loop will get executed and the statement inside the loop will be proessed. Here each time the iCounter value is increased one at a time till it reaches 16 and conditions becomes true the loop terminates.

When the above code is executed, it prints the following output in a message box.

The value of iCounter is : 11

The value of iCounter is : 12

The value of iCounter is : 13

The value of iCounter is : 14

The value of iCounter is : 15

The value of iCounter is : 16

b. The Do ... Loop Until Statements

Syntax:

Do

[block of code]

Loop Until [Condition]

<u>Example: Chapter 9.31 - DoUntil_Examp2.txt</u>

Sub DoUntil_Examp2()

Dim iCounter As Integer

  iCounter = 10

  Do

    iCounter = iCounter + 1

    MsgBox ("The value of iCounter is : " & iCounter)

  Loop Until iCounter < 15

End Sub

Here we have placed the Until part at the end. So this loop will execute at least once and the iCounter will be increased to 11. Once you reach the end of the loop the condition iCounter less than 15 is met ant the loop exits automatically.

When the above code is executed, it prints the following output in a message box.

The value of iCounter is : 11

Manipulating Objects and Collections

You will be spending a lot of time working with objects and collections. So you must know the most efficient ways to write your code to manipulate these objects and collections. VBA has two important constructs that can simplify working with objects and collections:

One is **For Each-Next constructs** which I have already explained in the For loop section. Second one is With-End With constructs.

With-End With constructs

The With-End With block instruction enables you to perform multiple operations on a single object. This enable the code to execute more quickly and code will be easy to read. Will look into an example for you to understand. First, we will write without using the **With-End With constructs.**

The following procedure formats the selected cells with the font 'Times New Roman', font size 16, Bold, Italic and the color Red.

Sub FontChange()

```vba
        Selection.Font.Name = "Times New Roman"
        Selection.Font.Size = 16
        Selection.Font.Bold = True
        Selection.Font.Italic = True
        Selection.Font.ColorIndex = 3
End Sub
```

The above procedure rewritten using a With-End With block will be like this.

Example: Chapter 9.32 - FontChange.txt

```vba
Sub FontChange ()

    With Selection.Font
        .Name = "Times New Roman"
        .Size = 16
        .Bold = True
        .Italic = True
        .ColorIndex = 3
    End With


End Sub
```

Using this type of block, your code is cleaner and easier to maintain. Whenever VBA executes it will go through one Object to the next lower object till it finds the method or property to execute separated by the notes. So more dots means more time to execute. In the first example all the lines start from Selection to the end.

After rewriting the code we have put the Selection object on top with the With-End With construct. As we have already defined the object with **With-End With constructs,** the Object is known to the VBA and it will execute faster. If there are less dots in the code the program will run faster.

Chapter 10

Error Handling

Error handling means programming practice of anticipating and coding for error conditions that may arise when your program runs. When we think an error is likely to occur at some point, it is good practice to add code to handle that situation. We usually refer to these errors as expected errors. If we don't have specific code to handle an error it is considered an unexpected error. We use the VBA error handling statements to handle the unexpected errors.

There are three types of errors in programming: (a) Syntax Errors, (b) Compiler errors (c) Runtime Errors, and (d) Logical Errors.

Syntax errors

Every language has a certain rule on how to code. In plain terms, we can say it is the grammar of the language. For example, the following line **Range("A1).value** causes a syntax error because it is missing a closing double quote at the end of A1 (should be like this Range("A1").value).

Sub Syntax_Error()

Dim x As String

x = Range("A1").value

End Sub

After you finish writing or editing a code and press return or move the cursor away, VBA immediately checks the statement for syntax and alerts you. If possible, it will solve the issue by itself.

Compiler Errors

VBA compiles the codes before executing the macro. Compiling means to change the code you typed to machine language the computer understands. For example, if you have not declared the variable even after you given Option Explicit at the beginning the code won't compile. Mostly these types of bugs are easy to spot and fix easily.

Run Time Errors

Runtime errors, also called exceptions, occur during execution of the program.

In the below example, this line **z = AddValue(x, y)** causes a runtime error; it is trying to call the function **AddValue**, which is not there. In fact, the function name is **AddVal**. Because of this typing mistake, we will be able to find this type of error during runtime only. Change the line to **z = AddVal(x, y)** and this program will work.

Example: Chapter 10.1 - Runtime_Error.txt

Sub Runtime_Error()

Dim x As Integer

Dim y As Integer

Dim z As Integer

x = 2

y = 5

z = AddValue(x, y)

MsgBox z

End Sub

Function AddVal(p As Integer, q As Integer)

AddVal = p + q

End Function

Logical Errors

Logical errors can be the most difficult type of errors to track down. These errors are not the result of a syntax or runtime error. Instead, they occur when you make a mistake in the logic that drives your script and you do not get the result you expected.

You cannot catch these errors easily because it depends upon the requirement of the program. For example, if you have made a function to return a number after specific calculations. Inside the complex calculation by mistake you have typed a minus sign instead of plus sign. Program will work but the logic will be wrong.

Handling Run Time errors

If you have no error handling code and a run time error occurs, VBA will display its standard run time error dialog box. It is ok to get these errors while developing the program but it should not be shown to the end user. The goal of well-designed error handling code is to anticipate potential errors, and correct them at run time or to end the program by giving a proper message. Your goal should be to prevent unhandled errors from arising.

The VBA On Error statement is used for error handling. This statement performs some action when an error occurs during runtime.

There are three different ways to use this statement.

On Error Goto 0 - the code stops at the line with the error and displays a message, is the default mode in VBA.

On Error Resume Next - the code moves to next line. No error message is displayed.

On Error Goto [label] - the code moves to a specific line or label. No error message is displayed. This is the one we use for error handling.

On Error Goto 0

When a run time error occurs, VBA displays its standard run time error message box, allowing you to go to debug mode or to terminate the VBA program by the user. So when you mention On Error Goto 0, it is the same as having no enabled error handler. Any error will cause VBA to display its standard error message box. In this scenario no error handling takes place.

Let's look into an example

Example: Chapter 10.2 - Runtime_Error1.txt

Sub Runtime_Error1()

Dim x As Integer

Dim y As Integer

x = 5

y = x / 0

End Sub

If you run this program, you will get an error like in the screenshot given below.

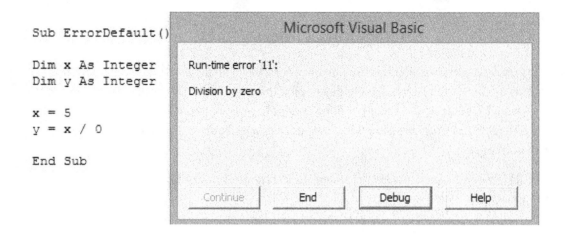

```
Sub ErrorDefault()

Dim x As Integer
Dim y As Integer

x = 5
y = x / 0

End Sub
```

When the error appears you can choose **End** or **Debug**

If you select End, then the application simply stops.

If you select Debug, the application stops on the error line as the screenshot below shows highlighting the error in yellow color.

```
    Sub ErrorDefault()

    Dim x As Integer
    Dim y As Integer

    x = 5
⇨   y = x / 0

    End Sub
```

When you are developing the program, this type of errors is good for debugging. But if you are developing for some other person you have to write codes to handle these errors and display a message in plain English. Or else the user thinks the program is full or bugs and it look unprofessional. For this, you must use **On Error Goto [label]** to give user-friendly error messages.

On Error Resume Next

This is the most commonly used and misused form. There are specific occasions when this is useful. Most of the time you should avoid using it.

It instructs to VBA to ignore the error and resume execution on the next line of code. On Error Resume Next does not fix the error, it instructs VBA to continue as if no error occurred. However, the error may cause problems, such as uninitialized variables or objects set to Nothing. So you must write the code to

163

test for an error condition and take appropriate action. You do this by testing the value of Err. Number and if it is not zero, execute appropriate code. For example,

On Error Resume Next

N = 1 / 0   ' cause an error

If Err.Number <> 0 Then

**   N = 1**

End If

This code attempts to assign the value 1 / 0 to the variable N. This is an illegal operation, so VBA will raise an error 11 -- Division By Zero -- and because we have On Error Resume Next in effect, code continues to the IF statement. This statement tests the value of Err.Number and assigns some other number to N.

On Error Goto [label]

If you specify a label whenever an error occurs, code execution immediately goes to the line following the line label. None of the code between the error and the label is executed, including any loop control statements.

Let's go through an example for you to understand.

Example: Chapter 10.3 - Runtime_Error2.txt

```
Sub Runtime_Error2()

On Error GoTo ErrHandler:

Dim nNum As Integer
Dim nResult As Integer

nNum = 10
nResult = 10 / 0
nResult = 10 / 4

MsgBox nResult

Exit Sub

ErrHandler:
MsgBox "Cannot perform divide by zero"

End Sub
```

Here we have declared two integer variables nNum and nResult. nNum we have assigned the value 10. nResult we are assigning the value 10 divided by 0. Division by zero will result an error. We have mentioned in the first line of code, On error you should go to the label **ErrHandler** and execute what is inside the label.

Once error has occurred the next line of codes will not get executed, means nResult = 10 / 4 and MsgBox nResult. It will go to the label ErrHandler mentioned at the end and execute what is inside that. There we have put a messagebox to give the answer Cannot perform divide by zero.

Instead of putting nResult = 10 / 0 if you write nResult = 10 / 5 the code will execute without any errors. Then you should put an Exit Sub before the Label for not executing the code mentioned in the ErrHandler. If there is no error then the code inside the label should not run. That is why I have used an Exit Sub before the label.

The label we use in the On...Goto statement, must be in the current Sub/Function. If not you will get a compilation error.

You can given any name to the label as per your choice.

The Resume Statement

The Resume statement instructs VBA to resume execution at a specified point in the code. You can use Resume only in an error handling block; any other use will cause an error. Moreover, Resume is the only way, aside from exiting the procedure, to get out of an error handling block. Do not use the Goto statement to direct code execution out of an error handling block. Doing so will cause strange problems with the error handlers.

The Resume statement has three forms:

Resume

Resume Next

Resume <label>

First form Resume

Used alone, **Resume causes execution to resume at the line of code that caused the error**. In this case, you must ensure that your error handling block fixed the problem that caused the initial error. Otherwise, your code will enter an endless loop, jumping between the line of code that caused the error and the error handling block.

The following code attempts to activate a worksheet that does not exist. This causes an error (9 - Subscript Out Of Range), and the code jumps to the error handling block which creates the sheet, correcting the problem, and resumes execution at the line of code that caused the error because I have mentioned the word Resume.

Example: Chapter 10.4 - Resume_Examp.txt

```
Sub Resume_Examp()

On Error GoTo ErrHandler:
Worksheets("NewSheet").Activate
Exit Sub

ErrHandler:

If Err.Number = 9 Then
  ' sheet does not exist, create a sheet.

  Worksheets.Add.Name = "NewSheet"

  ' go back to the line of code that caused the error
  Resume

End If

End Sub
```

Second form of Resume is Resume Next.

This causes **code execution to resume at the line immediately following the line which caused the error**. The following code causes an error (11 - Division By Zero) when attempting to set the value of N. The error handling block assigns 1 to the variable N and then execution resumes at the statement after the line that caused the error.

Example: Chapter 10.5 - ResumeNext_Examp.txt

```
Sub ResumeNext_Examp()

On Error GoTo ErrHandler:

N = 1 / 0

Debug.Print N

Exit Sub

ErrHandler:
N = 1
' go back to the line following the error
```

Resume Next

End Sub

Third form of Resume is Resume <label>:

This causes code execution to resume at a line label. This allows you to skip a section of code if an error occurs.

For example, this program will transform the execution to whatever codes are written in the Label ErrHandler if an error happens. It will not execute the line of codes written from where the error has occurred.

Example: Chapter 10.6 - Resume_Label.txt

```
Sub Resume_Label()
On Error GoTo ErrHandler:
   N = 1 / 0
    ' codes skipped if an error occurs
Label1:
MsgBox "Codes written inside Label1 will execute"
Exit Sub
ErrHandler:
    ' go back to the line at Label1:
    Resume Label1:
End Sub
```

Here we have specified in the label ErrHandler if the error occurs it should resume at Lable1, not at the line where the error has occurred. In the Label1 we have mentioned the codes to be executed.

Error Handling With Multiple Procedures

Every procedure need not have an error code. When an error occurs, VBA uses the last On Error statement to direct code execution. However, if the procedure in which the error occurs does not have an error handler, VBA looks backward through the procedure calls which lead to the erroneous code. For example, if procedure A calls B and B calls C, and A is the only procedure with an error handler, if an error occurs in procedure C, code execution is immediately transferred to the error handler in procedure A, skipping the remaining code in B.

Chapter 11

More Examples

Coloring maximum values

Example: Chapter 11.1 - MaxValueColoring.txt

```
Sub MaxValueColoring()

Dim lMaxValue As Double, rng As Range, cell As Range

Cells.Interior.ColorIndex = 0

Set rng = Range("A1").CurrentRegion

lMaxValue = WorksheetFunction.Max(rng)

For Each cell In rng

    If cell.Value = lMaxValue Then cell.Interior.ColorIndex = 22

Next cell

End Sub
```

In this example, we have created a macro to color the cell having the maximum value.

Here I have declared one variable lMaxValue as type Double and two Range objects rng and cell. Then we have added entire cells interior color to none. Why we are specifying the interior color to none at the beginning is to reset the background color to none if you are again running the procedure with new value.

We initialize rng with the numbers. For that, we use the CurrentRegion property from A1 cell. Whatever values are there it will be assigned to the rng Object variable.

Then we initialize lMaxValue with the maximum value of the numbers. We use the worksheet function Max to find the maximum value.

Finally, we color the maximum value. We use a For Each Next Loop to loop through each cell in the range in rng object variable.

Points to Note: instead of ColorIndex number 22 (red), you can use any ColorIndex number.

Hide sheet

This macro will hide sheet1.

Example: Chapter 11.2 - HideSheet.txt

Sub HideSheet()

Sheets("Sheet1").Visible = False

End Sub

You can also use index number of the sheet, **Sheets(1).Visible = False,** if you know the index number. One advantage of using the index number is if you change the sheet name to some other name still the program will hide the first sheet. This may be useful for hiding the information from the end user.

Department wise password

Here we have three departments HR, Admin, Finance and their data in sheet2. When the department gets the report, they should view only the data relating to them by entering the password given to them.

First, create an Excel sheet and enter the heading HR, Admin and Finance in A1, B1 and C1 cell of Sheet2. Fill the first four rows of each column with the data like this.

	A	B	C
1	HR	Admin	Finance
2	10	45	11
3	20	65	22
4	30	85	66

Then hide sheets sheet2 and sheet3. Now run this macro from a module.

Example: Chapter 11.3 - Hide Sheet 1.txt

Sub Hide_Sheet1()

Dim Dept As String

Dim InputPass As String

Dim Password(1 To 3) As String

Password(1) = "Recruite"

Password(2) = "Approval"

Password(3) = "Accounts"

```
Dept = InputBox("Please enter your department name")

InputPass = InputBox("Please enter the password")

If Dept = "HR" And InputPass = Password(1) Then

    Sheets(1).Range("A1:A4").Value = Sheets(2).Range("A1:A4").Value

End If

If Dept = "Admin" And InputPass = Password(2) Then

    Sheets(1).Range("A1:A4").Value = Sheets(2).Range("B1:B4").Value

End If

If Dept = "Finance" And InputPass = Password(3) Then

    Sheets(1).Range("A1:A4").Value = Sheets(2).Range("C1:C4").Value

End If

End Sub
```

This example is used to demonstrate how you can use VBA in various ways.

Changing Background colors

You can change the background color using Interior.ColorIndex Property. Here the number 5 denotes Blue 3 for Red, 4 for Green and 6 for Yellow. The ColorIndex property can generate up to 57 colors. You can see the full list from this link https://msdn.microsoft.com/en-us/library/cc296089(v=office.12).aspx.

Example: Chapter 11.4 - BackgoundColor.txt

```
Sub BackgoundColor()

Range("A1:C5").Interior.ColorIndex = 5 ' 5=Blue

End Sub
```


Change Font color and size

Example: Chapter 11.5 - FontColor.txt

To change the font color and font size of a particular Range. Hereby specifying the Font's ColorIndex property, you can change the color of the cells from A1:A3. Also if you use the size property of the font, you can change the size of the font.

Sub FontColor()

Range("A1:A3").Font.ColorIndex = 3 ' 3=Red

Range("A1:A3").Font.Size = 15

End Sub

Rename and Delete Worksheet

Example: Chapter 11.6 - RenameDelete.txt

Sub RenameDelete()

Sheets.Add

ActiveSheet.Name = "Temporary Sheet"

Sheets("Temporary Sheet").Delete

End Sub

Create New Workbook, Add Data, Save And Close The Workbook

Example: Chapter 11.7 - SaveandClose.txt

Sub SaveandClose()

Workbooks.Add

ActiveWorkbook.Sheets("Sheet1").Range("A1") = "Sample Data"

ActiveWorkbook.SaveAs "MyNewWorkbook.xls"

ActiveWorkbook.Close

End Sub

You can use Add method of a Workbooks object to add a new workbook. Then you can enter data in A1 cell and then use SaveAs to give a name and the close it.

It will save in the default folder; you can mention the full path as "c:\Temp\MyNewWorkbook.xls"

Insert And Delete Rows And Columns

Example: Chapter 11.8 - InsertandDelete.txt

Sub InsertandDelete()

Rows(6).Insert 'It will insert a row at 6 row

Rows(6).Delete 'it will delete the row 6

Columns("E").Insert 'it will insert the column at E

Columns("E").Delete 'it will delete the column E

End Sub

You can use Insert and Delete Properties of Rows to insert and delete rows. Also, you can use Insert and Delete Properties of Columns.

Row Height And Column Width

Example: Chapter 11.9 – HeightandWidth.txt

Sub HeightandWidth()

Rows(12).RowHeight = 33

Columns(5).ColumnWidth = 35

End Sub

You can increase and decrease the row height and column width with this macro.

Chapter 12

Debugging the Codes

Bugs

A bug is an error or flaw in a computer program, which produces an incorrect or unexpected result or causes it to behave in unintended ways. Given below are the leading causes of the bugs.

Incorrect Logic: You must have used a wrong logic to sort out the problem. You should think thoroughly before writing the codes.

Incorrect context bugs: This type of bugs appears when you attempt to do something at the wrong time like writing data to cells in the active sheet when the active sheet is a chart sheet.

Wrong data type bugs: This type of bugs occurs when you try to process data of the wrong type, such as attempting to take the square root of a text string.

Noncompatible version bugs: If you are using a feature in Excel 2016 and this feature will not work in Excel 2007. So you must develop programs keeping in mind to work in old versions also.

Beyond-your-control bugs: These are the most frustrating kind of bugs. For Example, a Microsoft upgrade with a minor change will make your macro useless.

Debugging

Debugging means to find out these bugs in the program you have written. Sometimes the Procedure or Function you have written may not work as intended. In this case, you have to find out what is wrong with the program. For that, you can use these strategies.

You should indent the code whenever necessary. If there are so many nested loops, then it will be easy to find out where the first loop begins and where the second loop starts with proper indentation. There is a button for that in the Edit toolbar under the view menu. Refer the image given below. First one is for indenting and the second one is for outdenting.

Also, keep your Sub and Function procedure simple and if it serves a single purpose, it is better. If your procedure has multiple things to do it is better you break down the procedure into multiple procedures and then call each procedure separately. In this way debugging and editing of the codes will be faster.

For example, you can write the main procedure like this.

Sub MainProc()

Call FirstProcedure

Call SecondProcedure

Call ThirdProcedure

End Sub

From the main procedure, you can call all the sub procedures and execute. In this way, it is easy to maintain and debug.

.

Msgbox Function

You can put Msgbox function wherever required to find out the value of a variable. Maybe you have designed the variable to hold a value but at run time the variable value may differ and programs output goes wrong. In this case, you can put Msgbox followed by the variable name to get a pop of the variable value at run time. Do not put too much Msgbox in the programs as it will be very annoying and then you have to figure out what each message box is.

We will look through an Example.

Example: Chapter 12.1 - RowColumnNum.txt

Sub RowColumnNum()

Dim columnNumber As Long
Dim rowNumber As Long

columnNumber = ActiveCell.Column
rowNumber = ActiveCell.Row

MsgBox columnNumber
MsgBox rowNumber

End Sub

Here we have given two Message boxes, one for displaying the Active cell column number and one for the row. For testing purpose, you can call this procedure from another procedure to get the column and row number of the active cell. Suppose if the calling procedure stops at the wrong cell, then you can easily find out the wrong logic.

Message box can be used to display the variable value at runtime. Also, you can display two variables in a single message box. Add one more with a & operator like this, MsgBox columnNumber & " " & rowNumber.

Or you can use the vbNewLine in between the variable, built in constant to display the variables in the next line.

Breakpoint

You can set breakpoints in the code by moving the cursor to the statement you want to halt execution. For that choose Debug Toggle Breakpoint (or press F9). Or else you can click the left side bar in the code window against the statement to insert a breakpoint. You will get a big brownish dot in the side bar and the code will also be highlighted in brown. If you want to remove the breakpoint, click the brown dot once more or select debug clear all break points from the menu or press Ctrl + Shift + F9. Once in breakpoint, you can step through the procedure. In the image given below, I have inserted two break points.

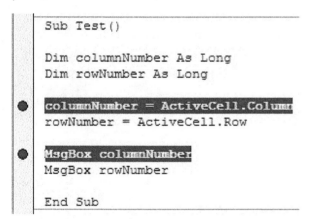

```
Sub Test()

Dim columnNumber As Long
Dim rowNumber As Long

columnNumber = ActiveCell.Column
rowNumber = ActiveCell.Row

MsgBox columnNumber
MsgBox rowNumber

End Sub
```

If you run this, procedure will execute till the line before the breakpoint and halt. Again you have to click run to run the program and again it will halt at the next breakpoint.

The good thing about breakpoint is you can hover the cursor above each variable and see what each variable is holding while executing the program. Run this program from your end and look at the variables during each breakpoint by hovering the cursor. This is very helpful while debugging. See the image given below; you can see the column number value when you hover the mouse while in the break point.

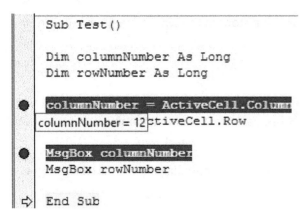

```
Sub Test()

Dim columnNumber As Long
Dim rowNumber As Long

columnNumber = ActiveCell.Column
columnNumber = 12ctiveCell.Row

MsgBox columnNumber
MsgBox rowNumber

End Sub
```

If you want to execute one line by line after the breakpoint or you want to execute the program one line at a time from the start of the procedure, press F8 to step through the procedure line-by-line.

Also if you use F8 for executing the code, the breakpoint will not work, it will execute one line of code if you keep on pressing F8.

You can clear all the breakpoints using the keyboard shortcut Ctrl + Shift + F9 or else you can click Debug > Clear all Breakpoints.

Permanent Breakpoints

One feature of breakpoints is they are not saved when you close a workbook. So if you come back to your program next day, you won't have any breakpoints that you have set. So use the STOP statement where you want to set a permanent breakpoint. So when the program reaches the stop statement, it will immediately stop as in this image given below.

```
Sub Test()

Dim columnNumber As Long
Dim rowNumber As Long

Stop

columnNumber = ActiveCell.Column
rowNumber = ActiveCell.Row

MsgBox columnNumber
MsgBox rowNumber

End Sub
```

Debug.Print

Use Debug.print followed by one or more variable value in your code to write values to the VBE Immediate window (if the immediate window is not visible press Ctrl + G). For example, if you want to monitor a value inside a loop, use something like the following procedure:

Example: Chapter 12.2 - Debug_Print.txt

Sub Debug_Print()

Dim i As Integer
For i = 1 To 10
Debug.Print "i " & i
Next
End Sub

In the Immediate window, you will get the variable values printed like this.

i 1

I 2

i 3

i 4

i 5

i 6

i 7

i 8

i 9

i 10

Here we are printing the value of the variable to the immediate window from 1 to 10. I have given the variable name in double quotes to see which variable is printed. You can check more variables like this.

If you have more variable, you can put a comma in between and use Debug.print like this

Debug.Print I, Myvariable, Lastrow

You can display as many variables as you like with a single Debug.Print statement.

More about Immediate Window and its uses

1. Get Information about The Active Workbook

The simplest use of the immediate window is to quickly get information about the workbook that you currently opened and active in the background. You can evaluate any line of VBA code in the Immediate Window, and it will immediately give you the result.

For example, to find out how many sheets are in the active workbook, type the following line of code in the immediate window and then press the Enter key.

?Activeworkbook.Worksheets.Count

The answer will be displayed on the next line of the immediate window, directly under the code.

Putting the question mark (?) at the beginning of the statement tells the immediate window that we are asking a question, and expecting a result.

You can ask questions like this.

?Range("A1").Value you will get the value of A1 cell.

Or if you type ?Range("A1").Value = 58 and if the value of A1 cell is 58, you will get the answer True.

Or if you type ?Activecell.Interior.Color you will get the number of the color 16777215.

2. Execute one line of Codes for testing

You can execute one line of codes from immediate window.

Type Range("A1").Value = 100 in immediate window and press Enter. Value in the A1 cell will become 100.

Type Range("A1").Font.Color = RGB(255, 0, 0) in immediate window and press Enter. Font color in the A1 cell will become red.

While writing the programs, you may not be sure about some codes outcome. So you can use these one-line codes to test the result of codes instead of writing a test macro for that. And once you check it, you can include the same in the main code. This kind of testing will save a lot of time; you can trust me on that.

3. Run a macro with Arguments

A macro cannot be run from within the procedure if it contains arguments. However, you can call the macro from the Immediate Window.

For arguments that are string variables (text), you will need to wrap the variable in quotation marks.Otherwise to test the macros with arguments you have to write a macro that supplies these arguments.

Example: Chapter 12.3 - Examp.txt

Sub Examp(first As String)

MsgBox ("this is testing " & first)

End Sub

In this example, we have created a procedure with arguments. So instead of writing a procedure to test the macro you type the procedure name and the string like this Examp "hi" in the immediate window.

4. Get or Set a Variable's Value

The Immediate Window can also be used to get answers about the procedure (macro) that is currently running. If you are stepping through your code (F8) or add a break point (F9) or add a STOP line in your code, then the code will pause. When the code is paused, you can use the Immediate Window to get information about any variables or objects that are referenced in the code.

You can get the variable value by hovering the mouse point over the variables, or you can type a question mark followed by the variable name and press Enter.

Also, you can change the variable value by entering the variable name followed by the equal sign and value and press Enter, like this, Variable = 20 (Variable is the variable name you give).

5. F8 – for line by line execution

As mentioned in the Breakpoint section you can execute the macro line by line by pressing F8. You can also use the menu, Debug > Step into, but the shortcut will be much faster. When you press F8 you will see a yellow line in the code, that line will be executed next when you press F8.

6. Skipping lines

You can skip lines of code while you are pressing F8. Click the small yellow arrow on the left bar and drag the arrow down the line and the macro will execute from there, skipping the lines in between. You can also drag the arrow up also.

7. Run to Cursor

Run to Cursor is just like another breakpoint, but in this case, you don't need to start debugger manually. When you select the run to cursor option, the debugger starts automatically and executes the lines of code before the selected line.

Go to Debug menu and select Run to Cursor or press the shortcut Ctrl + F8. Then you can press F8 from there for executing the procedure one line by one or press F5 to run the whole procedure.

8. The Locals Window

The locals window allows you to view the value of all the variables in a procedure when you are stepping through the procedure by pressing F8. To display the Locals window, choose Locals Window from the View menu. Using the Locals window is easier to display variable values than examining the value from the Immediate window. For simple variable types (e.g., Long and String variables), the value is displayed on one line. For complex types or objects (e.g., a Range variable), its properties are displayed in a collapsible tree-like structure.

9. The Watch Window

A watch is a variable or expression that has been placed in the window to enable you to monitor its value. Let's you watch the values of variables and expressions as your code executes.

The Watch window displays all the Watches in effect. You can display the Watch window by choosing Watch Window from the View menu. A Watch is an instruction to VBA to pause code when an expression is True or when the variable being watched changes value. To create a Watch on a variable, open the Watch window and right-click in the Watch window and choose Add Watch from the popup menu or choose Add Watch from the Debug windows. In the Add Watch dialog, enter in the Expression text box a variable name whose value you want to watch. Then choose Break When Value Changes. When you run the code, execution will pause at the line after the line that modifies the variable's value. When code pauses, the value of the variable will have already been updated.

Example: Chapter 12.4 - WatchExample.txt

```
Sub WatchExample()

Dim i As Integer

For i = 1 To 50
Range("A" & i).Value = i
Next i

End Sub
```

181

In the above example, we can set watch if the variable reaches 25. Click Watch window from the view menu. You will get Watches window. Add a watch by right clicking the watches window and in the Expression column type i = 25.

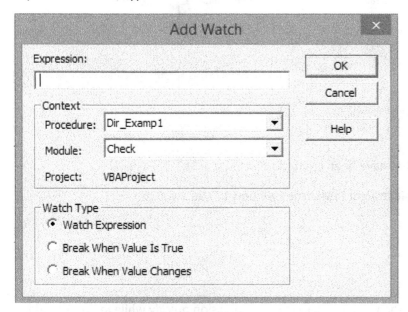

Please refer the image. You can change the Procedure name and Module from the Context menu. In the watch type below, you can change Watch Expression, adds the expression so the value can be watched during execution, same as Local Window. Break when value is true and Break when value changes.

Here you change the Watch type to Break when value is True. This will stop the execution when the variable value is 25. Once in break mode, you can check all the other variable values.

To remove a Watch, right-click in the Watch window and choose Delete Watch from the popup menu. To modify a Watch, right-click in the Watch window and choose Edit Watch from the popup menu.

When your application enters break mode, the watch expressions you select appear in a window allowing you to observe their values. It is also possible to set up conditional watches.

This window is automatically updated after each line of code is executed.

Watches Window

Although it is labeled as Watch Window, the actual window displays Watches Window. Given below is the image.

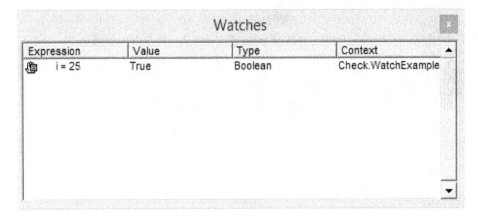

This window shows all the watches that have been created.

You can highlight a variable and drag it straight in Watches window to add a watch.

10. Quick Watch

This is a feature you can use to check the value of a variable or expression quickly while in break mode. Place the insertion point over the variable name and select (Debug > Quick Watch) or press (Shift + F9). You will get the variable value in a pop-up menu. From the quick watch window you can add the variable to watches window also. Try using this feature when you are in debug mode.

11. The Call Stack

The Call Stack is a data structure in VBA that tracks which procedure called another procedure. For example, if procedure AAA calls BBB which calls CCC, the Call Stack window will display the list of procedures starting with the most recent procedure at the top followed by the chain of procedures that were executed to get to the current position.

You can view the Call Stack by:

Use the menu option (View > Call Stack).

Using the shortcut key (Ctrl + L).

Use the Call Stack button on the Debug toolbar

Using the expand button on the Locals window dialog box

This is useful to track the flow of execution that ended up in the current location. Unfortunately, there is no programmatic way to get information from the call stack.

Keep in mind you can display the Call Stack dialog box only when you are in debug mode.

Example: Chapter 12.5 - CallStackExample.txt

Sub A()

Call B

End Sub

Sub B()

Call C

End Sub

Sub C()

MsgBox "In c"

End Sub

Don't run this program by clicking F5 instead use the F8 key to get into debug mode to execute the program one line by one till you reach third procedure C. Now view the call Stack. You can see the chain of execution.

You can double-click on any procedure name and in the code will that procedure will be shown with a green arrow. Else you can highlight the procedure and press the Show button.

12. Bookmarks

It is possible to insert bookmarks into your code. You can insert bookmarks within your VBA code from (Edit > Bookmarks). It makes it easy to return to a particular position in your code. It is indicated by a small blue square in the left margin of the code.

Bookmarks are not saved when the file is closed. They only exist in your open file. You can go through the bookmarks from edit Bookmarks. You can go to next bookmark, previous bookmark and also clear all the bookmarks from edit BookMarks.

Chapter 13

Add-Ins creation in Excel

Now you know how to write programs in VBA and you have written some good procedures, Sub as well as Function. Suppose your colleague wants these programs then it will be easy to make an add-in and give it rather than setting up a personal workbook and copy the code which is time-consuming.

Add-in has these advantages.

1. Easy to distribute the programs you created using the add-in. You have to create an add-in file and install it on their computer. All the programs will be available after installation of add-in.

2. You can set a password for the codes you have written while you create the add-in. This will make the casual user from looking into the code you have written.

3. Add-in will load along with Excel and will function along with Excel. The user will not be aware that an add-in is loaded.

4. If you have created a new function and integrated into an add-in it will work like any other function (Sum or Average or Max) of Excel. Suppose if you have created a function called FindComm then you can directly use the function like =FindComm(A1:A15) if you have installed the add-in. Otherwise, you have to type with the file name where the function is stored like this =MyFunctions.XLSM!FindComm(A1:A15).

Points to note: The Workbook you are going to create add-in must contain at least one worksheet and all the worksheets of the add-in will be hidden when converted to add-in. This worksheet of the add-ins can be used for calculation purpose if you want. You can, however, write code that copies all or part of a sheet from your add-in to a visible workbook.

We will go through an example with the steps for creating the add-in. Here we are creating a simple function to display the commission percentage for the sales done. If it is above or equal to five, it will display 10% and below five it will display 5%. Also, we have a Procedure to insert borders which is also added to the add-in.

1. First, open an Excel file and open Visual basic editor from the developer tab.

2. In the VBE go to Project Explorer. If it is not visible use Ctrl + R keyboard shortcut or select from view menu.

3. In the Project Explorer go to the Excel file you have just opened and right click any of the sheets object and insert a module. If you want you can rename the module.

4. Now paste the codes given below to this new module (both Commission function and InsertBorders Procedure)

Function Commission(ComVal As Long)

If (ComVal >= 5) Then
Commission = "10%"

Else
Commission = "5%"

End If

End Function

Sub InsertBorders()

Selection.Borders.LineStyle = True

End Sub

5. Now if you want to give a keyboard shortcut to the procedure InsertBorders, you can do it now before saving it as an add-in. Got to View tab in Excel and select the InsertBorders from the Macros and click options and assign the keyboard shortcut Ctrl + Shift + B.

6. Next, we have to save this file as add-in file. But before saving the add-in you must recompile the code. Otherwise it will take a little longer time to run first time. Select Debug > Compile from VBE to compile the code. Then select File > Save as to save it as an add-in.

Change the file type to Microsoft Excel Add-in (*.xla) for 97 to 2003 versions of Excel or xlam for an Excel 2007 or later onwards Excel from the "Save as Type" drop-down. The folder path will change automatically to the default folder path for your add-ins. It will usually be any of these depends upon the version of the Excel.

Excel 2016 - C:\Users\"user name"\App Data\Roaming\Microsoft\Addins\

Excel 2013 - C:\Users\"user name"\App Data\Roaming\Microsoft\Addins\

Excel 2010 - C:\Documents and Settings\"user name"\Application Data\Microsoft\Addins\

Excel 2007 - C:\Documents and Settings\"user name"\Application Data\Microsoft\Addins\

If you want, you can save the add-in to a different directory other than the Excel default directory. Give a name to the add-in and click save.

6. Once it is saved you can install the add-in you have just saved. Go to Developer –> Add-ins –> Excel Add-ins. In the Add-ins dialogue box, browse and locate the file that you saved, and click ok and add-in will get installed automatically.

Now you have successfully created an add-in file and installed the add-in. Now you don't want the Excel file you have just created the add-in. You can discard it if you want.

Now open an Excel sheet and type 4 in A1 cell and 15 in A2 cell. Now in the adjacent cell B1 type = Commission(A1) and press enter. You will see instantly you get the value 5% and copy this function to B2 and you will get 10%. Refer the image given below.

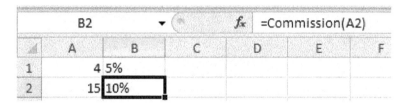

See the power of creating the add-in. This new function behaves exactly as the built-in functions of Excel and it will save huge amount of your time.

If the add-in contains a function then by installing the add-in, it will be available in the Excel. But if the add-in contains any procedures you can link this procedure with Quick access toolbar to make it easily available. Remember we have just copied InsertBorders procedure along with the Commission function.

Right click on any of the ribbon tabs and select Customize Quick Access Toolbar. In the Excel Options dialog box, Select Macros from the Choose commands from the drop-down. You'll notice that the macro **InsertBorders** is listed there. Click on the InsertBorders Macro and click Add. This will add the macro to the list on the right. If you want you can change the icon by clicking modify and then click OK. This will add the macro to the Quick Access Toolbar.

Now to run this code in any workbook, select cell or cells and click on the macro icon in the QAT.

Otherwise, if you have assigned the keyboard shortcut Ctrl + Shift + B to the procedure **InsertBorders,** then you can use this shortcut to call the procedure. For testing purpose select some cells and execute this procedure, all the selected cells will have borders.

More about Add-in creation

You can give the add-in a title and a description of yours. Before saving it as add-in file go to File > Properties and click the down arrow to get the advance properties. Select Summary Tab and fill the details. Summary tab will look like the image below.

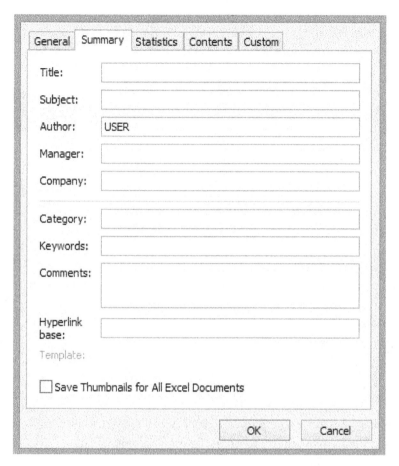

The title or name of your add-in is the name that will appear in the (Tools > Add-ins) dialog box and if no name is specified, the file name is used. The description is the short description that will appear at the bottom of the (Tools > Add-ins) dialog box. You can give a description in the Comments box before saving it as add-in to appear as description in (Tools > Add-ins) dialog box.

Protect the code from viewing

If you don't want others to see or modify the code written by you, you should protect it using password. This is for intellectual property or for not stealing the codes written by you. But Excel protection ability is pathetic. A person with correct VBA password recovery tool can easily open a protected sheet and also so many third party tools are available on the net for this purpose. So person who has the correct knowledge can view the code written by you. Before saving the file as add-in protect your code. For that, in VBE go to (Tools > VBAProject Properties)(Protection tab). You will get the properties window like this in image given below.

Check the checkbox "Lock project for viewing" and enter the password to lock the project. Once you have entered and saved the password next time when you try to open the module, you will be prompted for a password.

You can password protect the code even if you are not making an add-in. In this case, you can still execute the code from the macro window as the name of the macro will be visible but you will not be able to view the code without the password.

IsAddin Property

Every workbook has an IsAddin property which defines whether a workbook is just a workbook or an add-in. This can be viewed from the Workbook Properties window in the Visual Basic Editor.

This property is False for a normal workbook but is automatically set to True when the workbook is saved as an add-in.

When this property is True it means the workbook is always hidden and also means the workbook can be loaded using the (Tools > Add-ins) dialog box.

The advantage of having the worksheets hidden is that they can contain information which the add-in can both use and edit.

Editing of Add-in

If you want to edit the add-in you can make the changes directly. There is no need for the original Workbook from which you have created the add-in. Go to Visual basic in the Developer tab click on the Add-in name and open the module and make the changes (you will be prompted for the password if the password is there). Once you edit the add-in save your changes before closing the Excel file as you will not be prompted for saving.

To display the worksheets within an add-in after it has been created set the "IsAddin" property of the "ThisWorkbook" object to False, after you have made your changes set it back to True.

Converting an Add-in back to a Workbook

You can also convert an Excel Add-in back into a workbook. Change the "IsAddin" property to False and then resave the file using (File > Save As) as a regular workbook (".xls").

Please keep a note.

Any procedures in an Add-in are not displayed in the (Tools > Macro > Macros) dialog box.

When the "IsAddin" property is set to True the workbook is automatically excluded from the Workbooks() collection.

Reducing the size of an Add-in

You can remove all the comments of the code to reduce the size of the add-in as much as possible. It will help to reduce the file size as the add-ins should be as small as possible. The smaller the size, the faster it loads.

If you want other persons to use the add-in you have created give a copy of the add-in file and get it installed in there Excel. If you mail the workbook to someone else you will have to mail them the Add-In too!

Excel's Add-In Manager

The list contains the names of all add-ins that Excel knows about, and check marks identify installed add-ins. The image given in the next section.

Installing and Uninstalling add-in

You can open (install) and close (uninstall) add-ins from this dialog box by selecting or deselecting the check boxes (refer the image given below).

Go to Excel options and click Add-ins and on the right hand side, you can see Manage Excel add-in drop down list. Click go to open the Add-in manager and then browse to see all the add-ins available. You can select that add-in you want and click ok to install it.

If you want to install the add-in in your colleagues computer, copy the add-in you want and put it in their add-in folder. Open Add-ins manager as mentioned just now and click browse and paste the add-in you have copied and then select the add-in and click ok to install.

If you want to un-install the add-in go to Add-ins manager and simply untick the add-in you want to remove. Given below is the Add-ins manager screen shot. Only two Add-ins are installed, rest is not installed.

When you uninstall an add-in, it is not removed from your system. It remains on the list in case you want to install it later. Use the Browse button to locate additional add-ins and add them to the list if you want. If you want to completely remove the add-in file, first uninstall the add-in and then select the add-in file and delete.

Help Files for the Addins created

If you are want to create a helpfile for the add-in, you can resort to any of these.

Provide a Word File separately.

Provide as Cell comments.

Provide a text box control.

Provide a separate worksheet within the application.

Provide a HTML file which you can create in Excel itself.

Context-based help.

Make your own help system by using third party tools.

Conclusion

Hope you have enjoyed my book Excel Macros. If you have enjoyed this book and found it useful, please write a review of this book on Amazon.

I go through the reviews seriously and always go through them to improve my book and myself. By giving reviews, you are helping me provide better content that you will love in the future. A review doesn't have to be long, just one or two sentences and a number of stars you find appropriate (hopefully 5 of course). Also, if I think your review is useful, I will mark it as 'helpful'.

Once again thank you for reading this book.

Example file can be downloaded from ExceltoVBA.com

About the Author

Hi, my name is Vijay Kumar and I 'am crazy about learning as well as teaching Excel. This book is a compilation of the knowledge I have acquired by teaching as well learning Excel from the past ten years.

My Other Books

1. Excel Shortcuts: 130 Shortcuts that will change your life forever

This book covers various shortcuts from Basic to Advance level in Formatting, Data editing, Selection, Navigation and other useful shortcuts with examples.

These are some of the benefits of learning Shortcuts.

- Increase your productivity by speeder execution of tasks.
- Will increase the accuracy of the work you are doing.
- Help to get Raises and Promotion.
- To impress your Boss and Colleagues.
- It is fun to use the shortcuts.

2. Excel Formulas: 140 Excel Formulas and Functions with usage and examples

Do you want to know more about the Excel Formulas then this book is for you?

This book provides more than 140 Formulas and there uses with example workbook for you to understand and use it in your day to day work.

3. Vlookup Mastery: Learn Vlookup Hlookup and Index Match In-Depth

This book is specifically written for the lookups function in Excel. This book covers advanced concepts in Vlookup, Hlookup and Index Match functions.

If you know these three functions in depth, then all the database capabilities of the Excel can be utilized to its fullest capability.

Each chapter contains example files for you to practice along while you read this book. By implementing the techniques specified in this book you will save a huge amount of time.

All the example files are explained in detail with simple data.

I can definitely say this book will address so many problems you face with the Lookup functions.